Everyday COOKING

VOLUME 9

DIABETIC LIVING® EVERYDAY COOKING
IS PART OF A BOOK SERIES PUBLISHED BY
BETTER HOMES AND GARDENS SPECIAL
INTEREST MEDIA, DES MOINES, IOWA

Steak and Chimichurri Salad,
recipe, *p. 49*

From the Editors

If one of your biggest challenges each day is gathering your family around the table for a healthful meal, this new edition of fresh and light recipes is just for you. Each recipe includes complete nutrition information so you can track your calories, carbs, fat, and sodium and make sure you are targeting your meal plan.

You'll find eye-opening breakfast fare such as up-scale but easy Peach 'n' Cream Crepes, *p. 120*, and grab-and-go Pumpkin-Apple Smoothies, *p. 117*. For a twist tradition, check out Pork Paprikash with Cauliflower "Rice," *p. 26*, and Buffalo-Spiced Steak Salads with Blue Cheese Dressing, *p. 49*. And for everything in between, look for main-dish soups, veggie-fresh side dishes, satisfying snacks, and delicious desserts.

You can count on these recipes. Each has been thoroughly tested and has received the Better Homes and Gardens® Test Kitchen seal of approval for accuracy, ease of preparation, and great taste. Your family will love these meals, and you will relish the pleasure of serving homemade, nutritious food.

On the Cover:
Carnitas Tacos,
recipe, *p. 27*

Photographer: Jacob Fox
Food Stylist: Jennifer Peterson

21

102

146

Everyday COOKING VOLUME 9

CONSUMER MARKETING

Vice President, Consumer Marketing	STEVE CROWE
Consumer Marketing Product Director	HEATHER SORENSEN
Consumer Marketing Product Manager	WENDY MERICAL
Business Manager	DIANE UMLAND
Production Manager	AL RODRUCK
Billing/Renewal Manager	TAMI BEACHEM
Contributing Project Manager	SHELLI MCCONNELL, PURPLE PEAR PUBLISHING, INC.
Contributing Photographer	JACOB FOX
Contributing Food Stylist	JENNIFER PETERSON
Test Kitchen Director	LYNN BLANCHARD
Test Kitchen Chef	CARLA CHRISTIAN, RD, LD
Administrative Assistant	LORI EGGERS

SPECIAL INTEREST MEDIA

Editorial Content Director	DOUG KOUMA
Assistant Managing Editor	JENNIFER SPEER RAMUNDT

DIABETIC LIVING® MAGAZINE

Editor	JENNIFER WILSON
Creative Director	MICHELLE BILYEU
Senior Associate Editor	CAITLYN DIIMIG, RD
Associate Editor	BAILEY MCGRATH
Art Director	NIKKI SANDERS

MEREDITH NATIONAL MEDIA GROUP

President JON WERTHER

Chairman and Chief Executive Officer STEPHEN M. LACY

Vice Chairman MELL MEREDITH FRAZIER

In Memoriam — E.T. MEREDITH III (1933-2003)

Diabetic Living® Everyday Cooking is part of a series published by Meredith Corp., 1716 Locust St., Des Moines, IA 50309-3023.

If you have comments or questions about the editorial material in *Diabetic Living® Everyday Cooking,* write to the editor of *Diabetic Living* magazine, Meredith Corp., 1716 Locust St., Des Moines, IA 50309-3023. Send an e-mail to *diabeticlivingmeredith.com* or call 800/678-2651. *Diabetic Living®* magazine is available by subscription or on the newsstand. To order a subscription to the magazine, go to *DiabeticLivingOnline.com*

CONTENTS

**Salmon Burgers with Coleslaw
and Roasted Carrots**
recipe, *p. 92*

1

FAMILY-PLEASING
DINNERS

Make dinner a family affair with easy weeknight offerings, such

as Grilled Salmon with Veggie Packets, Seared Pork Chops with

Apples and Onion, and Baked Chicken Taquitos. You'll find an

assortment of recipes for the grill, leisurely oven bakes, fast

stir-fries, and fix-and-forget slow cooker dishes.

Skillet Fajitas

Skillet Fajitas

38 g CARB

SERVES 4
HANDS ON 25 min.
TOTAL 40 min.

- 2 tsp. salt-free fiesta lime seasoning
- 1 tsp. garlic powder
- ⅛ tsp. salt
- ⅛ tsp. black pepper
- 1 lb. skinless, boneless chicken breast halves, cut into thin strips
- 2 tsp. canola oil
- 2 cups green, yellow, and/or red sweet pepper strips
- 1 large onion, thinly sliced
- 8 6-inch 100% whole wheat flour tortillas
- ½ cup refrigerated salsa
- ¼ cup snipped fresh cilantro
- ¼ cup plain fat-free Greek yogurt (optional)
- ¼ cup refrigerated avocado dip (guacamole) (optional)
- 1 lime, cut into 4 wedges

1. In a plastic bag combine lime seasoning, garlic powder, salt, and black pepper. Add chicken strips, several at a time, shaking to coat.
2. In a 12-inch cast-iron skillet heat 1 tsp. of the oil over medium. Add chicken; cook 3 to 4 minutes or until no longer pink, stirring frequently. Remove chicken.
3. In skillet heat remaining 1 tsp. oil over medium. Add sweet peppers and onion; cook 8 to 10 minutes or until tender and golden, stirring frequently. Stir in chicken; heat through. Meanwhile, heat tortillas as directed on package.
4. Serve chicken mixture in tortillas with the remaining ingredients.

PER SERVING (2 fajitas each) **CAL** 359, **FAT** 9 g (3 g sat. fat), **CHOL** 83 mg, **SODIUM** 588 mg, **CARB** 38 g (6 g fiber, 6 g sugars), **PRO** 33 g

Black Bean and Corn Salad recipe, p. 99

Baked Chicken Taquitos

Baked Chicken Taquitos

17 g CARB

SERVES 4
HANDS ON 10 min.
TOTAL 25 min.

- 2 cups shredded cooked chicken breast
- ½ cup shredded reduced-fat cheddar cheese (2 oz.)
- ¼ cup taco sauce
- 1 tsp. ground cumin
- 8 6-inch corn tortillas

1. Preheat oven to 425°F. Line a baking sheet with parchment paper.
2. For filling, in a bowl combine chicken, cheese, taco sauce, and cumin.
3. Stack tortillas and wrap in damp paper towels. Microwave about 40 seconds or until warm and softened. Spread filling onto the bottom thirds of tortillas. Tightly roll up tortillas. Place, seam sides down, on the prepared baking sheet.
4. Bake about 15 minutes or until edges of tortillas are starting to brown.

PER SERVING (2 taquitos each) **CAL** 242, **FAT** 7 g (3 g sat. fat), **CHOL** 70 mg, **SODIUM** 239 mg, **CARB** 17 g (3 g fiber, 3 g sugars), **PRO** 27 g

Chicken and Gnocchi
with Asparagus

Chicken and Gnocchi with Asparagus

32 g
CARB

SERVES 4
HANDS ON 30 min.
TOTAL 40 min.

- 1 cup low-sodium chicken broth
- 2 Tbsp. all-purpose flour
- ¼ tsp. black pepper
- ⅛ tsp. salt
- 1 lb. asparagus, trimmed and cut diagonally into 1½-inch pieces
  Nonstick cooking spray
- 2 cups shelf-stable whole wheat potato gnocchi
- 1 tsp. olive oil
- 12 oz. skinless, boneless chicken breast halves, cut into bite-size pieces

- ½ of an 8-oz. pkg. reduced-fat cream cheese (neufchatel)
- 1 Tbsp. snipped fresh oregano

1. Preheat oven to 450°F. In a bowl whisk together broth, flour, pepper, and salt.

2. Place asparagus in a single layer on a large baking sheet lined with foil; coat lightly with cooking spray. Roast 8 to 10 minutes or until asparagus is crisp-tender, turning once or twice.

3. Meanwhile, cook gnocchi in boiling water according to package directions. Drain, reserving ¼ cup of the cooking water.

4. Coat a 12-inch nonstick skillet with cooking spray. Pour oil into skillet; heat over medium-high. Add chicken;

cook 5 to 6 minutes or until chicken is no longer pink and starting to brown, stirring frequently.

5. Stir broth mixture and cream cheese into chicken in skillet. Cook and stir until sauce is thickened, adding enough of the reserved gnocchi cooking water to thin sauce if needed. Cook and stir 1 minute more. Stir in cooked gnocchi and oregano; heat through. If desired, sprinkle individual servings with additional fresh oregano leaves.

PER SERVING (¾ cup chicken mixture + ½ cup asparagus each) **CAL** 330, **FAT** 11 g (4 g sat. fat), **CHOL** 75 mg, **SODIUM** 585 mg, **CARB** 32 g (3 g fiber, 2 g sugars), **PRO** 26 g

Moroccan-Spiced Chicken and Swiss Chard

15 g
CARB

SERVES 4
HANDS ON 25 min.
TOTAL 1 hr. 40 min.

- 4 5-oz. skinless, boneless chicken breast halves
- 3 Tbsp. lemon juice
- 1 Tbsp. olive oil
- ¾ tsp. ground turmeric
- ¾ tsp. ground cumin
- ¾ tsp. ground cinnamon
- ¼ tsp. salt
- ¼ tsp. black pepper
  Nonstick cooking spray
- 2 cloves garlic, minced
- 14 cups stemmed and coarsely chopped Swiss chard (about 12 oz.)
- 1 to 2 Tbsp. water (optional)
- ¼ cup chopped pitted dried plums (prunes)
- 2 Tbsp. balsamic vinegar
- ¼ cup coarsely chopped pistachio nuts, toasted

1. Place chicken in a resealable plastic bag set in a shallow dish. For marinade, in a bowl whisk together the next five ingredients (through cinnamon) and ⅛ tsp. each of the salt and pepper. Pour marinade over chicken. Seal bag; turn to coat chicken. Marinate in the refrigerator 1 to 8 hours, turning bag occasionally. Drain chicken, discarding marinade.
2. Grill chicken, covered, over medium heat 12 to 15 minutes or until chicken is no longer pink (165°F), turning once.
3. Meanwhile, coat a 12-inch skillet with cooking spray; heat over medium-high. Add garlic; cook and stir 30 seconds. Add Swiss chard; cook 2 to 4 minutes or just until chard is wilted but tender, stirring frequently and adding the water if needed to moisten. Remove from heat. Sprinkle with the remaining ⅛ tsp. each salt and pepper. Stir in dried plums and vinegar.
4. Spoon Swiss chard mixture onto a platter. Top with chicken and pistachios.

Moroccan-Spiced Chicken and Swiss Chard

PER SERVING *(1 chicken breast half + ½ cup Swiss chard mixture each)* **CAL** 291, **FAT** 11 g (2 g sat. fat), **CHOL** 91 mg, **SODIUM** 582 mg, **CARB** 15 g (4 g fiber, 7 g sugars), **PRO** 34 g

QUICK TIP Cara Cara oranges look like navel oranges but have pink flesh. They contain 20% more vitamin C and nearly 30% more vitamin A than regular oranges.

Orange Chicken and Barley

Orange Chicken and Barley

38 g
CARB

SERVES 4
HANDS ON 20 min.
TOTAL 45 min.

- 3 Cara Cara or navel oranges
- 1½ cups reduced-sodium chicken broth
- ¾ cup quick-cooking barley
- 2 cups fresh snow pea pods, trimmed and thinly bias-sliced
- 2 Tbsp. canola oil
- 1 Tbsp. snipped fresh mint
- 2 tsp. Dijon-style mustard
- ½ tsp. salt
- ¼ tsp. black pepper
- 1 lb. skinless, boneless chicken breast halves, cut into bite-size strips
  Nonstick cooking spray
- 2 cups sliced fresh mushrooms

1. Remove 1 tsp. zest from an orange. Peel and section oranges over a bowl to catch juices; reserve 2 Tbsp. juice.
2. In a large saucepan bring broth to boiling; stir in barley. Simmer, covered, 10 to 12 minutes or until tender. Remove from heat. Stir in pea pods. Let stand, covered, 5 minutes; drain if necessary. Stir in oil, mint, mustard, ¼ tsp. of the salt, and ⅛ tsp. of the pepper. Stir in orange sections and the reserved orange juice.
3. Sprinkle chicken with the remaining ¼ tsp. salt and ⅛ tsp. pepper. Coat a 10-inch nonstick skillet with cooking spray; heat over medium. Add chicken; cook and stir until no longer pink. Remove from skillet. Add mushrooms to skillet; cook about 5 minutes or until tender and beginning to brown, stirring occasionally.
4. To serve, stir chicken and mushrooms into barley mixture. Sprinkle servings with orange zest.

PER SERVING (1½ cups each) **CAL** 369, **FAT** 11 g (1 g sat. fat), **CHOL** 83 mg, **SODIUM** 611 mg, **CARB** 38 g (7 g fiber, 12 g sugars), **PRO** 33 g

Creamy Spinach and Artichoke Chicken

Creamy Spinach and Artichoke Chicken

40 g
CARB

SERVES 6
HANDS ON 25 min.
SLOW COOK 4 hr. (low)

- 1 lb. skinless, boneless chicken breast halves, cut crosswise into 1-inch-wide strips
- 1 9-oz. pkg. frozen artichoke hearts, thawed and cut up
- 2 large onions, cut into wedges
- 1 medium red sweet pepper, cut into thin bite-size strips
- 1 10.75-oz. can reduced-fat and reduced-sodium condensed cream of chicken soup
- ⅓ cup water
- 1 tsp. dried Italian seasoning, crushed
- ¼ tsp. salt
- ¼ tsp. black pepper
- 4 oz. reduced-fat cream cheese (neufchatel), cut into cubes
- 3 cloves garlic, minced
- 3 cups fresh baby spinach
- 6 oz. dried wide whole wheat noodles, cooked according to pkg. directions

1. In a 3½- or 4-qt. slow cooker combine chicken, artichokes, onions, and sweet pepper. In a bowl combine the next five ingredients (through black pepper). Pour over chicken mixture in cooker.
2. Cover and cook on low 4 to 5 hours.
3. Stir cream cheese and garlic into mixture in cooker. Cover and let stand 5 minutes. Stir until cream cheese is melted and smooth. Stir in spinach leaves. Serve chicken mixture over noodles.

PER SERVING (1⅓ cups chicken mixture + ⅔ cup noodles each) **CAL** 323, **FAT** 8 g (3 g sat. fat), **CHOL** 64 mg, **SODIUM** 474 mg, **CARB** 40 g (8 g fiber, 9 g sugars), **PRO** 25 g

Braised Chicken Thighs and Vegetables with Polenta

43 g CARB

SERVES 4
HANDS ON 20 min.
TOTAL 35 min.

- ½ tsp. dried oregano, crushed
- ½ tsp. ground cumin
- ¼ tsp. salt
- ¼ tsp. ground turmeric
- ⅛ tsp. cayenne pepper
- 4 large skinless, boneless chicken thighs (about 1½ lb. total)
- 1 Tbsp. vegetable oil
- ⅓ cup reduced-sodium chicken broth
- 1 lb. baby carrots
- 1 recipe Polenta
- 3 cups torn fresh kale

1. Stir together the first five ingredients (through cayenne pepper). Sprinkle chicken with spice mixture. In a large nonstick skillet cook chicken in hot oil over medium-high 5 to 8 minutes or until browned, turning once. Remove from skillet. Add broth and carrots to skillet. Bring to boiling; reduce heat. Simmer, covered, 5 minutes. Return chicken to skillet. Simmer, covered, about 15 minutes or until chicken is done (at least 170°F) and carrots are just tender.

2. Meanwhile, make Polenta. Add kale to skillet. Bring to boiling; reduce heat. Simmer, uncovered, over medium about 5 minutes or until liquid is slightly reduced and vegetables are hot. Serve chicken and vegetables with Polenta.

Polenta In a medium saucepan bring 3 cups water to boiling. In a bowl combine 1 cup cornmeal, ¼ tsp. salt, and ¼ tsp. black pepper; stir in 1 cup cold water. Slowly add cornmeal mixture to boiling water in saucepan, stirring constantly. Cook and stir until mixture returns to boiling. Cook, uncovered, over low about 5 minutes or until thick and cornmeal is tender, stirring occasionally. Stir in ¼ cup fat-free milk.

PER SERVING *(1 chicken thigh + 1 cup polenta + ¾ cups vegetables)* **CAL** 435, **FAT** 11 g (2 g sat. fat), **CHOL** 160 mg, **SODIUM** 572 mg, **CARB** 43 g (6 g fiber, 7 g sugars), **PRO** 40 g

Spicy Grits with
Greens and Sausage

Spicy Grits with Greens and Sausage

51g
CARB

SERVES 6
TOTAL 45 min.

Nonstick cooking spray
8 oz. uncooked bulk Italian turkey sausage
1 cup bottled roasted red sweet peppers, drained and cut into thin strips
1 cup chopped onion
1 Tbsp. canola oil
6 cups water
2 tsp. finely chopped canned chipotle chile pepper in adobo sauce (tip, p. 64)
¾ tsp. kosher salt
¼ tsp. black pepper

2 cups quick-cooking (hominy) grits
3 cups coarsely chopped kale or fresh spinach
¾ cup light sour cream
6 Tbsp. shredded reduced-fat Colby and Monterey Jack or reduced-fat cheddar cheese (1½ oz.)
Crushed red pepper (optional)

1. Coat a 12-inch nonstick skillet with cooking spray; heat skillet over medium. Add sausage; cook until browned. Stir in roasted red peppers; heat. Using a slotted spoon, transfer sausage mixture to a small bowl. Cover and keep warm.
2. Add onion and the oil to skillet. Cook and stir 4 to 5 minutes or until

tender, stirring and scraping up browned bits from bottom of skillet. Add the water, chipotle pepper, salt, and black pepper to skillet. Bring to boiling. Gradually stir in grits; stir in kale. Reduce heat to low. Cook, uncovered, about 5 minutes or until thick, stirring frequently. Remove from heat. Stir in ½ cup of the sour cream.
3. Spoon grits into dishes. Sprinkle with cheese. Top with sausage mixture and remaining sour cream. If desired, sprinkle with crushed red pepper.

PER SERVING *(1½ cups each)* **CAL** 368, **FAT** 11 g (4 g sat. fat), **CHOL** 39 mg, **SODIUM** 568 mg, **CARB** 51 g (4 g fiber, 4 g sugars), **PRO** 15 g

Asian Meatball Stir-Fry

Asian Meatball Stir-Fry

37 g
CARB

SERVES 4

TOTAL 15 min.

½ cup canned pineapple tidbits (juice pack), undrained
¼ cup rice wine vinegar
1 tsp. cornstarch
½ tsp. ground ginger
2 tsp. canola oil
12 cooked teriyaki-flavor chicken meatballs

8 oz. baby bok choy, cut into thin wedges
1 cup bite-size red sweet pepper strips
2 containers (2 cups) cooked multigrain rice medley, heated

1. Drain pineapple, reserving ¼ cup. of the juice; set pineapple aside. For sauce, in a small bowl stir together pineapple juice and the next three ingredients (through ginger).

2. In a 12-inch nonstick skillet heat oil over medium-high. Add meatballs; cook and stir 3 minutes. Add bok choy and sweet pepper; cook and stir 2 to 3 minutes or until vegetables are crisp-tender.

3. Stir sauce; pour into skillet. Add pineapple. Cook and stir until thickened and bubbly. Serve with rice.

PER SERVING (¾ cup stir-fry + ½ cup rice medley each) **CAL** 307, **FAT** 13 g (2 g sat. fat), **CHOL** 60 mg, **SODIUM** 552 mg, **CARB** 37 g (5 g fiber, 12 g sugars), **PRO** 13 g

Mexican Stuffed Acorn Squash

29 g CARB

SERVES 6
HANDS ON 15 min.
TOTAL 1 hr. 15 min.

- 3 1¼-lb. acorn squash, halved and seeded
  Nonstick cooking spray
- ¾ tsp. salt
- ¼ tsp. black pepper
- 2 Tbsp. canola oil
- 12 oz. 93% lean ground turkey
- ¾ cup chopped green sweet pepper
- ½ cup chopped onion
- 1¼ cups cubed yellow summer squash
- 1 14.5-oz. can no-salt-added diced tomatoes, drained
- 1 tsp. salt-free fiesta lime seasoning
- ¼ tsp. crushed red pepper (optional)
- 6 Tbsp. crumbled queso fresco
- 3 Tbsp. snipped fresh cilantro

1. Preheat oven to 400°F. Pour ½ inch water into a large roasting pan; add acorn squash, cut sides down. Bake 30 minutes. Turn squash halves cut sides up; coat with cooking spray and sprinkle with ¼ tsp. of the salt and the black pepper. Bake 20 to 25 minutes more or until tender.
2. Meanwhile, in a 10-inch nonstick skillet heat 1 Tbsp. of the oil over medium. Add ground turkey; cook until browned. Remove turkey.
3. In skillet heat remaining 1 Tbsp. oil over medium. Add sweet pepper and onion; cook 5 to 7 minutes or until onion is tender, stirring occasionally. Add summer squash; cook and stir 3 minutes or just until squash is tender. Stir in turkey, remaining ½ tsp. salt, and the next three ingredients (through crushed red pepper); heat through.
4. Spoon turkey mixture into squash cavities. Bake 10 minutes. Top with queso fresco and cilantro.

PER SERVING *(1 stuffed squash half each)*
CAL 262, **FAT** 11 g (3 g sat. fat), **CHOL** 47 mg, **SODIUM** 419 mg, **CARB** 29 g (5 g fiber, 4 g sugars), **PRO** 15 g

Mexican Stuffed
Acorn Squash

Molasses-Mustard Marinated Flank Steak

10 g
CARB

SERVES	4
HANDS ON	25 min.
TOTAL	4 hr. 50 min.

1 lb. beef flank steak
⅓ cup molasses
2 Tbsp. spicy brown mustard
2 Tbsp. olive oil
1 Tbsp. water
2 cloves garlic, minced
¼ tsp. caraway seeds, crushed
¼ tsp. black pepper
⅛ tsp. salt
2 medium tomatoes, cored and cut into 1-inch-thick slices
1 medium red onion, cut into ½-inch-thick slices
Nonstick cooking spray
¼ tsp. salt
4 lemon wedges

1. Trim fat from steak. Score both sides of steak in a diamond pattern by making shallow diagonal cuts at 1-inch intervals. Place steak in a large resealable plastic bag. For marinade, in a bowl whisk together molasses, mustard, 1 Tbsp. of the oil, the water, garlic, caraway seeds, ⅛ tsp. of the pepper, and the ⅛ tsp. salt. Add marinade to bag with steak. Seal bag, turning to coat steak. Marinate steak in the refrigerator 4 to 24 hours, turning bag occasionally.

2. Remove from the refrigerator 15 minutes before cooking. Drain steak, discarding marinade. Lightly coat tomato and onion slices with cooking spray.

3. Grill steak and tomato and onion slices, covered, over medium heat. Grill tomato slices 4 to 6 minutes or until just browned, turning once. Grill onion slices 8 to 10 minutes or until just tender, turning once. Grill steak 15 to 18 minutes for medium (160°F), turning once.

4. Transfer steak to a cutting board; cover with foil and let stand 10 minutes. Thinly slice steak across the grain.

5. Sprinkle tomato and onion slices with the remaining ⅛ tsp. pepper and the ¼ tsp. salt . Drizzle with the remaining 1 Tbsp. olive oil. Serve with sliced steak and lemon wedges.

PER SERVING (3 oz. cooked meat + 1½ tomato slices + 1 onion slice each) **CAL** 242, **FAT** 11 g (3 g sat. fat), **CHOL** 70 mg, **SODIUM** 262 mg, **CARB** 10 g (1 g fiber, 8 g sugars), **PRO** 25 g

Molasses-Mustard Marinated Flank Steak

Beef-and-Vegetable
Stir-Fry

Beef-and-Vegetable Stir-Fry

27g
CARB

SERVES 4

TOTAL 35 min.

8 oz. boneless beef sirloin steak
⅓ cup cold water
2½ tsp. cornstarch
3 Tbsp. reduced-sodium
 soy sauce
1 Tbsp. dry sherry or reduced-
 sodium chicken broth
⅛ tsp. salt
 Nonstick cooking spray
4 tsp. vegetable oil
2 cloves garlic, minced
2 tsp. grated fresh ginger
1 medium onion, cut into thin
 bite-size strips
½ cup thinly sliced carrot
½ cup thinly sliced celery
½ to 1 fresh jalapeño chile
 pepper, seeded and finely
 chopped (tip, p. 64)

1 cup thin bite-size strips green
 and/or red sweet pepper
1 cup sliced fresh mushrooms
1 small zucchini, halved
 lengthwise and thinly sliced
 (1 cup)
1⅓ cups hot cooked brown rice
2 Tbsp. chopped dry-roasted
 unsalted peanuts or toasted
 unsalted cashews
2 Tbsp. snipped fresh basil or
 parsley (optional)

1. If desired, partially freeze meat for easier slicing. Trim fat from meat. Thinly slice meat across the grain into bite-size strips. For sauce, in a bowl stir together the cold water and cornstarch; stir in soy sauce, dry sherry, and salt. Set meat and sauce aside.

2. Coat a 10-inch nonstick skillet with cooking spray; heat over medium-high. Add 2 tsp. of the oil. Add garlic and ginger; cook and stir 15 seconds.

Add onion, carrot, celery, and chile pepper to hot skillet. Cook and stir 3 minutes. Add sweet pepper; cook and stir 1 minute. Add mushrooms and zucchini; cook and stir 3 to 4 minutes more or just until vegetables are crisp-tender. Remove vegetables from skillet.

3. Add the remaining 2 tsp. oil to hot skillet. Add meat strips; cook and stir 1 to 2 minutes or until browned. Stir sauce; stir into meat in skillet. Cook and stir until thickened and bubbly. Return cooked vegetables to skillet, stirring to coat. Cook and stir 1 minute more. Serve with hot cooked rice. Sprinkle with peanuts and, if desired, basil.

PER SERVING *(1 cup stir-fry + ⅓ cup rice each)* **CAL** 275, **FAT** 10 g (2 g sat. fat), **CHOL** 34 mg, **SODIUM** 548 mg, **CARB** 27 g (4 g fiber, 6 g sugars), **PRO** 18 g

Enchilada Tostadas

35 g
CARB

SERVES 8
HANDS ON 25 min.
TOTAL 45 min.

- 1 recipe Enchilada Sauce
- 8 6-inch 100% whole wheat flour tortillas
  Nonstick cooking spray
- 1 lb. 90% lean ground beef
- 1 15-oz. can reduced-sodium black beans, rinsed and drained
- 1 cup cooked brown rice
- ⅓ cup water
- 2 Tbsp. salt-free taco seasoning
- 2 cups shredded romaine lettuce
- 1 cup chopped roma tomatoes
- 1 cup plain fat-free Greek yogurt
- ½ cup thinly sliced radishes
- ½ cup snipped fresh cilantro

1. Prepare Enchilada Sauce. Meanwhile, preheat oven to 400°F. Coat both sides of tortillas with cooking spray and place on two large baking sheets. Bake 8 to 10 minutes or until crisp and golden, turning once and rotating pans halfway through baking.

2. Coat a 10-inch nonstick skillet with cooking spray; heat over medium-high. Add ground beef; cook until browned. Drain off any fat. Stir in beans, rice, the water, and taco seasoning. Cook until thick and heated through, stirring occasionally.

3. Spoon ½ cup meat mixture onto each tortilla. Drizzle with sauce and top with the remaining ingredients.

Enchilada Sauce In a small saucepan heat 2 tsp. canola oil over medium. Stir in 2 tsp. all-purpose flour; cook and stir 1 minute. Stir in 2 tsp. chili powder and 1 tsp. dried oregano, crushed; cook and stir 30 seconds more. Stir in one 8-oz. can no-salt-added tomato sauce, ¾ cup water, and ½ tsp. salt. Bring to boiling; reduce heat. Simmer, uncovered, 8 to 10 minutes or until slightly thick, stirring occasionally.

PER SERVING *(1 tostada each)* **CAL** 302, **FAT** 10 g (3 g sat. fat), **CHOL** 37 mg, **SODIUM** 499 mg, **CARB** 35 g (7 g fiber, 5 g sugars), **PRO** 22 g

Enchilada Tostadas

Blistered Beans and Beef

17 g
CARB

SERVES 4
TOTAL 35 min.

- 2 Tbsp. cider vinegar
- 3 Tbsp. reduced-sodium soy sauce
- 1 Tbsp. packed brown sugar
- ¼ tsp. crushed red pepper
- 8 oz. boneless beef sirloin
- 6 tsp. canola oil
- 2 cloves garlic, minced
- 1 lb. fresh thin green beans, trimmed
- 2 cups sliced stemmed fresh shiitake mushrooms
- ½ cup sliced red onion
  Hot cooked rice noodles or rice (optional)
- 1 recipe Pickled Radishes

1. For sauce, in a bowl stir together the first four ingredients (through crushed red pepper). Trim fat from meat. Thinly slice across the grain into bite-size strips.
2. In a 12-inch wok or skillet heat 2 tsp. oil over medium-high. Add garlic; cook and stir 30 seconds. Add beef; cook and stir 2 minutes. Remove from wok.
3. Heat 2 tsp. oil in wok over medium-high. Add half the beans; cook and stir 3 minutes. Remove from skillet. Add remaining 2 tsp. oil and remaining beans; cook and stir 3 minutes. Return all beans to skillet. Add mushrooms and onion; cook and stir 2 to 3 minutes or until beans are blistered and onion is crisp-tender. Return beef and any accumulated juices to skillet. Add sauce; stir to coat. If desired, serve over rice noodles or rice. Top with Pickled Radishes.

Pickled Radishes In a bowl whisk together ¼ cup cider vinegar, 2 Tbsp. packed brown sugar, and ½ tsp. salt until sugar is dissolved. Stir in ½ cup very thinly sliced radishes. Let stand 30 minutes. Drain before using.

PER SERVING (1¼ cups each) **CAL** 218, **FAT** 10 g (1 g sat. fat), **CHOL** 34 mg, **SODIUM** 534 mg, **CARB** 17 g (4 g fiber, 11 g sugars), **PRO** 17 g

QUICK TIP Substitute sweet pepper strips in one or two colors for the green beans if you like. And use button or cremini mushrooms instead of shiitake.

Blistered Beans and Beef

Barley Tabbouleh and Lebanese Meatballs

30 g
CARB

SERVES 6
HANDS ON 30 min.
TOTAL 1 hr. 50 min.

3½ cups unsalted chicken stock
1 cup hull-less barley or regular pearled barley
2 cups snipped fresh parsley
2 cups chopped unpeeled seedless cucumber
1 cup chopped tomatoes
½ cup finely chopped red onion
2 Tbsp. snipped fresh mint
¼ cup lemon juice
1½ Tbsp. olive oil
2 cloves garlic, minced
½ tsp. salt
¼ tsp. black pepper
1 recipe Lebanese Meatballs
¾ cup plain fat-free Greek yogurt (optional)

1. For tabbouleh, in a large saucepan combine broth and barley. Bring to boiling; reduce heat. Simmer, uncovered, 1 hour or until desired tenderness; drain. Transfer barley to a bowl and let cool. Stir in the next five ingredients (through mint). In another bowl whisk together the next five ingredients (through pepper). Add to barley mixture; toss to coat. Set aside at room temperature.
2. In a 12-inch nonstick skillet cook Lebanese Meatballs over medium 15 to 18 minutes or until browned and done (160°F), turning occasionally. Serve with tabbouleh. If desired, top with yogurt and additional mint.

Lebanese Meatballs In a bowl combine 12 oz. 90% lean ground beef; 2 Tbsp. each finely chopped onion and snipped fresh parsley; 1 Tbsp. snipped fresh mint; 1 clove garlic, minced; ½ tsp. each ground coriander and black pepper; and ¼ tsp. each ground cumin and salt; mix well. Form mixture into 12 meatballs.

PER SERVING *(2 meatballs + 1 cup tabbouleh each)* **CAL** 286, **FAT** 10 g (3 g sat. fat), **CHOL** 37 mg, **SODIUM** 406 mg, **CARB** 30 g (7 g fiber, 3 g sugars), **PRO** 19 g

Garlic-Lime Pork with Farro and Kale

Garlic-Lime Pork with Farro and Kale

27 g
CARB

SERVES 4
HANDS ON 10 min.
TOTAL 20 min.

3 Tbsp. lime juice
1 Tbsp. peanut butter or almond butter
1½ tsp. honey
¼ tsp. salt
1 1¼-lb. pork tenderloin
¼ tsp. black pepper
   Nonstick cooking spray
2 tsp. olive oil
2 tsp. minced garlic
1 8.5-oz. pkg. cooked farro
8 oz. pkg. prewashed cut kale
2 Tbsp. chopped walnuts, toasted (optional)
   Lime wedges (optional)

1. In a small bowl whisk together lime juice, peanut butter, honey, and salt. Trim fat from meat. Cut meat into 12 slices. Sprinkle with pepper.
2. Coat a 10-inch nonstick skillet with cooking spray; add 1 tsp. of the oil to skillet. Heat skillet over medium-high.

Add meat slices in a single layer; cook about 3 minutes or until browned. Turn meat; add the remaining 1 tsp. oil and the garlic. Cook until meat is browned and a thermometer registers 145°F. Remove meat from skillet; cover and keep warm.
3. Stir lime mixture into drippings in skillet. Add farro; cook and stir over medium until grains are separated. Add kale; cook and stir until mixture is heated through and kale is coated and beginning to soften. If desired, season to taste with additional pepper.
4. Top farro mixture with meat slices. If desired, garnish with walnuts and lime wedges.

Tip To toast nuts, spread in a shallow baking pan. Bake in a 350°F oven 5 to 10 minutes or until golden, shaking pan once or twice.

PER SERVING *(3 pork slices + ¾ cup farro mixture each)* **CAL** 333, **FAT** 10 g (6 g sat. fat), **CHOL** 88 mg, **SODIUM** 282 mg, **CARB** 27 g (3 g fiber, 4 g sugars), **PRO** 34 g

Seared Pork Chops with Apples and Onion

33 g
CARB

SERVES 4
HANDS ON 15 min.
TOTAL 40 min.

- 4 7- to 8-oz. bone-in pork center-cut rib chops, trimmed of fat
- ½ tsp. salt
- ½ tsp. black pepper
    Nonstick cooking spray
- 2 firm cooking apples, such as Gala or Fuji, cut into ¼-inch slices
- 1 large onion, cut into thin wedges
- 2 cloves garlic, minced
- ¼ cup dry white wine
- ¼ cup reduced-sodium chicken broth
- 1 to 2 tsp. Dijon-style mustard
- 1 tsp. butter
- 1⅓ cups hot cooked brown rice
- 1 Tbsp. fresh thyme leaves

1. Sprinkle chops with salt and pepper. Coat a 12-inch nonstick skillet with cooking spray; heat skillet over medium-high. Add chops; cook 4 to 5 minutes or until browned on both sides. Remove from skillet; keep warm.
2. In skillet combine apples, onion, and garlic. Cook over medium-high 6 to 8 minutes or until apples are golden, stirring occasionally. Carefully add wine; cook 1 to 2 minutes, stirring to scrape up crusty browned bits. Stir in broth, mustard, and butter. Return chops to skillet. Simmer, covered, 4 to 6 minutes or until a thermometer inserted in chops registers 145°F.
3. Serve chops and apple mixture with rice. Sprinkle with thyme.

PER SERVING (1 pork chop + ½ cup apple mixture each) **CAL** 321, **FAT** 7 g (3 g sat. fat), **CHOL** 69 mg, **SODIUM** 426 mg, **CARB** 33 g (4 g fiber, 12 g sugars), **PRO** 29 g

**Seared Pork Chops
with Apples and Onion**

Pork Paprikash with Cauliflower "Rice"

Pork Paprikash with Cauliflower "Rice"

24 g CARB

SERVES 4
HANDS ON 10 min.
TOTAL 30 min.

- 1 1-lb. pork tenderloin
- 6 cups chopped cauliflower (1½ lb.)
- 2 Tbsp. olive oil
- ⅛ tsp. salt
- 1 medium onion, cut into thin wedges
- 1½ Tbsp. paprika
- ½ tsp. black pepper
- ¼ tsp. salt
- 1 14.5-oz. can no-salt-added diced tomatoes with basil, garlic, and oregano, undrained
- 1 cup reduced-sodium chicken broth
- ¼ cup bottled mild banana peppers, finely chopped
- ⅓ cup light sour cream
- 2 Tbsp. all-purpose flour

1. Trim fat from meat. Cut meat into bite-size pieces. Place cauliflower in a food processor. Cover and pulse until cauliflower is evenly chopped into rice-size pieces.

2. In a 12-inch nonstick skillet heat 1 Tbsp. of the oil over medium-high. Add cauliflower and the ⅛ tsp. salt. Cook 8 to 10 minutes or until golden brown flecks appear throughout, stirring occasionally.

3. Meanwhile, in a 10-inch skillet heat the remaining 1 Tbsp. oil over medium-high. Add meat and onion; cook about 3 minutes or until meat is starting to brown, stirring occasionally. Sprinkle with paprika, black pepper, and ¼ tsp. salt. Cook and stir 1 minute more.

4. Add tomatoes, broth, and banana peppers. Bring to boiling; reduce heat to medium-low. Cook, covered, 5 minutes. Increase heat to medium-high. Cook, uncovered, 4 to 6 minutes or until slightly thickened, stirring frequently. In a small bowl stir together sour cream and flour; stir into meat mixture. Cook and stir until thickened and bubbly.

5. Serve meat mixture over cauliflower "rice." If desired, top each serving with additional 2 tsp. sour cream and a sprinkle of paprika.

PER SERVING *(1¼ cups meat mixture + 1 cup cauliflower "rice" each)* **CAL** 319, **FAT** 12 g (3 g sat. fat), **CHOL** 79 mg, **SODIUM** 593 mg, **CARB** 24 g (11 g fiber, 11 g sugars), **PRO** 31 g

Carnitas Tacos

28g CARB

SERVES 8
HANDS ON 30 min.
SLOW COOK 8 hr. (low)

- 1 3- to 3½-lb. bone-in pork shoulder roast
- ½ cup chopped onion
- ⅓ cup orange juice
- 1 Tbsp. ground cumin
- 1½ tsp. kosher salt
- 1 tsp. dried oregano, crushed
- ¼ tsp. cayenne pepper
- 1 lime
- 2 5.3-oz. cartons plain fat-free Greek yogurt
  Dash kosher salt
- 16 6-inch soft yellow corn tortillas
- 4 leaves green cabbage, quartered
- 1 cup very thinly sliced red onion
- 1 cup refrigerated salsa (optional)

1. Remove meat from bone; discard bone. Trim fat from meat. Cut meat into 2- to 3-inch pieces; place in a 3½- or 4-qt. slow cooker. Stir in the next six ingredients (through cayenne pepper).

2. Cover and cook on low 8 to 10 hours or high 4 to 5 hours. Remove pork from cooker. Shred pork using two forks. Stir in enough cooking liquid to moisten.

3. For lime crema, remove 1 tsp. zest and squeeze 2 Tbsp. juice from lime. In a small bowl combine lime juice, yogurt, and dash salt.

4. Serve pork in tortillas with cabbage, red onion, salsa (if desired), and lime crema. Sprinkle with lime zest.

PER SERVING *(2 tacos each)* **CAL** 301, **FAT** 8 g (2 g sat. fat), **CHOL** 69 mg, **SODIUM** 329 mg, **CARB** 28 g (4 g fiber, 7 g sugars), **PRO** 29 g

QUICK TIP Look for harissa paste, a fiery-hot Mediterranean seasoning, in the international section of large supermarkets.

Tunisian Roasted Vegetables with Tuna

Tunisian Roasted Vegetables with Tuna

9g CARB

SERVES	6
HANDS ON	20 min.
TOTAL	1 hr. 5 min.

Nonstick cooking spray
1 small head cauliflower, cut into 1-inch pieces (3 cups)
2 cups cherry tomatoes
2 yellow, red, and/or orange sweet peppers, cut into 1-inch pieces
2 Tbsp. red wine vinegar or sherry vinegar
2 tsp. harissa paste
1 tsp. caraway seeds, crushed
1 clove garlic, minced
¼ tsp. kosher salt
Dash black pepper
3 Tbsp. olive oil
1 12-oz. can chunk white tuna (water pack), drained and flaked
3 hard-cooked eggs, peeled, quartered, and halved
⅓ cup pitted Kalamata olives, halved

1. Preheat oven to 400°F. Coat a 15×10-inch baking pan with cooking spray. Spread cauliflower in the prepared baking pan. Roast 10 minutes. Add tomatoes and sweet peppers. Roast 20 minutes more, stirring once.
2. Meanwhile, for vinaigrette, in a small bowl combine the next six ingredients (through black pepper). Whisk in oil.
3. In a bowl combine tuna and 2 Tbsp. of the vinaigrette; toss gently to coat. Drizzle 3 Tbsp. of the vinaigrette over roasted vegetables; toss gently to coat. Roast 15 to 20 minutes more or until vegetables are tender and starting to brown.
4. Divide vegetables, tuna, eggs, and olives among individual plates. Drizzle with the remaining vinaigrette.

PER SERVING (½ cup roasted vegetables + 1½ oz. tuna + ½ of a hard-cooked egg each) **CAL** 189, **FAT** 11 g (2 g sat. fat), **CHOL** 112 mg, **SODIUM** 364 mg, **CARB** 9 g (3 g fiber, 5 g sugars), **PRO** 13 g

Pistachio-Crusted Baked Trout

Pistachio-Crusted Baked Trout

4g CARB

SERVES	4
HANDS ON	20 min.
TOTAL	35 min.

4 4- to 5-oz. fresh or frozen trout fillets, skinned
Nonstick cooking spray
½ tsp. coriander seeds
½ tsp. cumin seeds
½ tsp. caraway seeds
4 tsp. olive oil
1 tsp. lemon zest
1 clove garlic, minced
½ tsp. kosher salt
¼ tsp. ground cinnamon
¼ tsp. black pepper
¼ cup pistachio nuts, finely chopped
4 lemon wedges

1. Thaw fish, if frozen. Preheat oven to 350°F. Line shallow baking pan with foil and coat with cooking spray.
2. Heat a small saucepan over low; add coriander, cumin, and caraway seeds. Cook and stir 4 minutes or until fragrant and golden. (Do not allow the seeds to burn or they will taste bitter.) Remove from heat. Using a small food processor or mortar and pestle, grind seeds. Stir in the next six ingredients (through pepper).
3. Place pistachios in a small bowl. Rinse fish; pat dry with paper towels. Spread one side of fish fillets with spice mixture. Bringing up two opposite ends, fold fish into thirds. Dip tops and sides of fish bundles into nuts to coat; place in the prepared baking pan. Sprinkle with any remaining nuts.
4. Bake 15 to 20 minutes or until fish flakes easily. Serve with lemon wedges.

PER SERVING (1 fillet each) **CAL** 227, **FAT** 12 g (2 g sat. fat), **CHOL** 67 mg, **SODIUM** 283 mg, **CARB** 4 g (1 g fiber, 1 g sugars), **PRO** 25 g

Cilantro-Jalapeño Shrimp

Cilantro-Jalapeño Shrimp

24 g
CARB

SERVES 4	
HANDS ON 25 min.	
TOTAL 50 min.	

- 1 lb. fresh or frozen large shrimp in shells
- 3½ cups snipped fresh cilantro
- ½ cup lime juice
- 4 fresh jalapeño chile peppers, seeded if desired (tip, p. 64)
- ¼ cup olive oil
- 2 medium mangoes, halved, seeded, peeled, and cut into thin bite-size strips
- 6 oz. jicama, peeled and cut into thin bite-size strips (2 cups)
- ½ cup slivered red onion
- ½ cup thinly sliced cucumber
- ¼ tsp. salt

1. Thaw shrimp, if frozen. For marinade, in a food processor combine 3 cups of the cilantro, the lime juice, jalapeño peppers, and oil. Cover and process until smooth.

2. For mango salad, in a bowl combine the remaining ½ cup cilantro and the remaining ingredients. Stir in ¼ cup of the marinade. Cover and chill until ready to serve.

3. Meanwhile, peel and devein shrimp, leaving tails intact if desired. Rinse shrimp; pat dry with paper towels. Place shrimp in a resealable plastic bag set in a shallow dish. Pour the remaining marinade over shrimp. Seal bag; turn to coat shrimp. Marinate in the refrigerator 20 minutes. Drain shrimp, discarding marinade. Thread shrimp onto eight 10-inch skewers, leaving ¼ inch between pieces.

4. Grill kabobs, covered, over medium heat 4 to 6 minutes or until shrimp are opaque, turning once. Serve shrimp kabobs with mango salad.

Tip If using wooden skewers, soak them in water for at least 30 minutes; drain before using.

PER SERVING *(2 shrimp skewers + ½ cup mango salad each)* **CAL** 204, **FAT** 4 g (1 g sat. fat), **CHOL** 159 mg, **SODIUM** 269 mg, **CARB** 24 g (5 g fiber, 15 g sugars), **PRO** 22 g

Citrus Shrimp with Black Rice

29 g
CARB

SERVES	4
HANDS ON	20 min.
TOTAL	55 min.

- 2 oranges
- 1⅓ cups water
- ¾ cup uncooked black rice
- ¾ tsp. salt
- 1 lb. fresh or frozen peeled and deveined medium shrimp, thawed
- 2 Tbsp. olive oil
- 2 cloves garlic, minced
- ¼ tsp. black pepper
- 4 cups baby arugula
- Orange wedges (optional)

1. Remove 1 tsp. zest and squeeze ½ cup juice from the oranges. In a 2-qt. saucepan bring the water, rice, and ½ tsp. of the salt to boiling; reduce heat. Simmer, covered, about 30 minutes or until water is absorbed. Remove from heat and let stand 5 minutes. Stir in ½ tsp. of the orange zest and ¼ cup of the orange juice.

2. Meanwhile, rinse shrimp; pat dry. For marinade, in a bowl combine oil, garlic, pepper, and the remaining ½ tsp. orange zest, ¼ cup orange juice, and ¼ tsp. salt. Add shrimp; toss to coat. Cover with foil or plastic wrap and marinate in the refrigerator 10 minutes.

3. Heat a 10-inch skillet over medium. Add shrimp mixture; cook and stir about 5 minutes or until shrimp are opaque. Using a slotted spoon, remove shrimp from skillet. For sauce, bring marinade to simmering. Cook 1 to 2 minutes or until marinade is slightly thickened.

4. Spoon warm rice and shrimp over arugula and drizzle with sauce. If desired, serve with orange wedges.

PER SERVING *(3 oz. cooked shrimp + ½ cup rice + 1 cup arugula each)* **CAL** 290, **FAT** 9 g (1 g sat. fat), **CHOL** 183 mg, **SODIUM** 579 mg, **CARB** 29 g (2 g fiber, 4 g sugars), **PRO** 27 g

Citrus Shrimp with Black Rice

Grilled Citrus Scallops and Asparagus

20 g CARB

SERVES	4
HANDS ON	15 min.
TOTAL	30 min.

- 1 orange
- 1 lemon
- 2 lb. fresh asparagus, trimmed
- 2 Tbsp. olive oil
- ¼ tsp. kosher salt
- ¼ tsp. cracked black pepper
- 1½ lb. fresh sea scallops (about 12 large)
- ¾ tsp. lemon-pepper seasoning

1. Remove zest from orange and lemon. Cut orange and lemon into quarters.
2. In a bowl combine asparagus, 1 Tbsp. of the oil, the salt, and pepper.
3. Grill asparagus, covered, over medium heat 7 to 10 minutes or until crisp-tender, turning once. Remove from grill.
4. Meanwhile, rinse scallops; pat dry with paper towels. In a bowl combine scallops, the orange and lemon zests, the remaining 1 Tbsp. oil, and lemon-pepper seasoning. Marinate at room temperature 5 minutes.

5. Grease grill rack. Grill scallops, covered, over medium heat 8 to 10 minutes or until scallops are opaque, turning once. Add the orange and lemon quarters to grill the last 2 to 3 minutes of grilling or until grill marks appear, turning once.
6. Serve scallops with asparagus and grilled orange and lemon quarters.

Tip Place the asparagus spears perpendicular to the grates to keep them from falling through.

PER SERVING (3 scallops + 2½ oz. asparagus each) **CAL** 276, **FAT** 8 g (1 g sat. fat), **CHOL** 56 mg, **SODIUM** 409 mg, **CARB** 20 g (7 g fiber, 8 g sugars), **PRO** 34 g

Asian-Marinated Salmon

29 g CARB

SERVES	2
HANDS ON	30 min.
TOTAL	1 hr. 30 min.

- 2 4- to 5-oz. fresh or frozen salmon fillets
- 2 Tbsp. reduced-sodium soy sauce
- 1 Tbsp. water
- 1 Tbsp. honey
- 2 tsp. olive oil
- 1½ tsp. finely chopped bottled pickled sushi ginger
- ¼ tsp. prepared wasabi paste
- ¼ cup sliced carrots
- ¼ cup fresh snow pea pods, halved
- ½ cup fresh shiitake mushrooms, stems removed and caps sliced
- ½ cup shredded napa cabbage
- 1 cup cooked wild rice
- 2 Tbsp. sliced green onion

1. Thaw fish, if frozen. Rinse fish; pat dry with paper towels. Measure thickness of fish. Place fish in a resealable plastic bag set in a shallow dish.
2. For marinade, in a bowl stir together soy sauce, the water, honey, 1 tsp. of the oil, the ginger, and wasabi paste. Pour half of the marinade over fish. Seal bag; turn to coat fish. Marinate in the refrigerator 1 hour, turning bag occasionally. Chill the remaining marinade until ready to serve.
3. Preheat oven to 450°F. Line a shallow baking pan with parchment paper. Drain fish, discarding marinade. Place fish in the prepared baking pan. Tuck under any thin edges. Bake 4 to 6 minutes per ½-inch thickness of fish or until fish flakes easily.
4. Meanwhile, in a 10-inch nonstick skillet heat the remaining 1 tsp. oil over medium-high. Add carrots and pea pods; cook and stir 3 minutes. Add mushrooms and cabbage; cook and stir about 3 minutes more or until vegetables are tender. Stir in wild rice and the reserved chilled marinade; heat through. Serve fish over rice mixture. Sprinkle with green onion.

PER SERVING (1 salmon fillet + ¾ cup stir-fry each) **CAL** 330, **FAT** 12 g (2 g sat. fat), **CHOL** 62 mg, **SODIUM** 513 mg, **CARB** 29 g (3 g fiber, 9 g sugars), **PRO** 28 g

Grilled Citrus Scallops and Asparagus

Grilled Salmon with Veggie Packets

14 g
CARB

SERVES	4
HANDS ON	15 min.
TOTAL	27 min.

- 1 fennel bulb
- 4 cups broccoli florets
- 1 Tbsp. olive oil
- ½ tsp. salt
- ½ tsp. black pepper
- 4 4-oz. fresh salmon fillets with skin
- ½ cup fat-free sour cream
- 1½ Tbsp. lemon juice
- 1 Tbsp. snipped fresh parsley

1. Cut stalks and root end off fennel bulb, reserving the wispy fronds. Halve, core, and thinly slice fennel. Snip the fennel fronds.

2. Tear off a 22×18-inch sheet of heavy foil. Place fennel slices and broccoli in the center of foil. Drizzle with oil and sprinkle with ¼ tsp. each of the salt and pepper; toss to coat. Bring up long edges of foil and seal with a double fold. Fold the ends to enclose vegetables, leaving space for steam to build.

3. Rinse salmon; pat dry with paper towels. Sprinkle with the remaining ¼ tsp. of the salt and pepper.

4. Grease grill rack. Grill foil packet and salmon, covered, over medium heat until vegetables in packet are tender (open one end carefully to check doneness) and salmon flakes easily, turning once. (Allow 12 to 15 minutes for vegetables and 4 to 6 minutes per ½-inch thickness for salmon.)

5. Meanwhile, for sauce, in a bowl stir together sour cream, lemon juice, parsley, and 1 tsp. of the snipped fennel fronds.

6. Serve salmon with vegetables and sauce. If desired, top with additional snipped fennel fronds.

PER SERVING (1 salmon fillet + ¾ cup vegetables + 2 Tbsp. sauce each) **CAL** 256, **FAT** 11 g (2 g sat. fat), **CHOL** 65 mg, **SODIUM** 436 mg, **CARB** 14 g (2 g fiber, 2 g sugars), **PRO** 26 g

Grilled Salmon with Veggie Packets

Stuffed Tilapia Rolls

6g CARB

SERVES 4
HANDS ON 30 min.
TOTAL 50 min.

- 4 4- to 5-oz. fresh or frozen tilapia fillets
- ¼ cup water
- 2 cloves garlic, minced
- 2 cups fresh baby spinach
- 1 egg white, lightly beaten
- ¾ cup crumbled goat cheese (chèvre) (3 oz.)
- ½ cup soft bread crumbs
- 2 Tbsp. pine nuts, toasted
- 2 Tbsp. plain fat-free Greek yogurt
- 1½ tsp. lemon zest
- 1 tsp. paprika
- ½ cup dry white wine

1. Thaw fish, if frozen. Preheat oven to 400°F. Rinse fish; pat dry.

2. In a 10-inch skillet bring the water and garlic to boiling. Add spinach; reduce heat to medium. Cook, covered, 2 to 3 minutes or until spinach is wilted. Cool slightly; squeeze out excess liquid.

3. For stuffing, in a bowl combine the next six ingredients (through lemon zest). Stir in cooked spinach.

4. Arrange fish, skinned sides down, on a work surface; sprinkle with paprika. Turn fish skinned sides up. For each fish roll, spoon about ¼ cup of the stuffing onto a short end of the fillet. Roll up fillet to enclose stuffing; secure with a toothpick if necessary. Place fish rolls, seam sides down, in a 2-qt. shallow baking dish.

5. Pour wine into the bottom of baking dish. Bake, covered, 20 to 25 minutes or until fish flakes easily. To serve, spoon cooking liquid over fish.

PER SERVING *(1 roll each)* **CAL** 270, **FAT** 11 g (5 g sat. fat), **CHOL** 73 mg, **SODIUM** 229 mg, **CARB** 6 g (1 g fiber, 1 g sugars), **PRO** 31 g

Tofu and Noodle Stir-Fry

41 g
CARB

SERVES 4	
HANDS ON 25 min.	
TOTAL 40 min.	

4 oz. dried brown rice noodles
1 12.3-oz. pkg. light firm silken-style tofu, cut into ¾-inch cubes
3 Tbsp. lime juice
2 Tbsp. white miso paste
1 Tbsp. honey
1 Tbsp. reduced-sodium soy sauce
2 tsp. grated fresh ginger
¼ to ½ tsp. crushed red pepper
Nonstick cooking spray
2 Tbsp. canola oil
½ cup sliced green onions, white parts only
2 cloves garlic, minced
1 cup fresh mung bean sprouts
2 cups thin bite-size strips peeled jicama
1 Tbsp. white sesame seeds, toasted

1. Prepare rice noodles according to package directions; drain. Place tofu cubes on a paper towel-lined plate.
2. In a small bowl whisk together the next six ingredients (through crushed red pepper).
3. Coat a 10-inch nonstick skillet with cooking spray. Heat 1 Tbsp. of the oil in skillet over medium-high. Add tofu; cook 6 to 8 minutes or until golden brown, turning once. Remove tofu from skillet; cover and keep warm.
4. In the same skillet heat the remaining 1 Tbsp. oil over medium. Add green onions and garlic; cook and stir 4 minutes. Add bean sprouts; cook and stir 1 to 2 minutes. Stir in lime juice mixture, cooked tofu, and jicama. Cook 1 to 2 minutes more or until heated through. Stir in rice noodles. Sprinkle each serving with sesame seeds.

Tip To brown the tofu thoroughly on two sides, add the tofu cubes to the hot oil in a single layer. Cook, without stirring, until bottoms of tofu are golden brown. Using tongs, gently turn tofu cubes over. Cook, without stirring, until golden brown.

PER SERVING *(1½ cups each)* **CAL** 282, **FAT** 10 g (1 g sat. fat), **CHOL** 0 mg, **SODIUM** 454 mg, **CARB** 41 g (5 g fiber, 9 g sugars), **PRO** 10 g

Pasta, Broccoli, and Red Bean Toss

48g
CARB

SERVES 4
HANDS ON 15 min.
TOTAL 30 min.

- 4 oz. dried medium shell pasta or desired pasta
- 5 cups broccoli florets
- 1 15-oz. can no-salt-added red kidney beans, undrained
- 1 Tbsp. olive oil
- 1 cup chopped onions
- ¼ tsp. salt
- ½ cup reduced-sodium chicken broth
- 1½ tsp. chili powder
- ½ cup finely shredded Parmesan cheese
- ¼ cup snipped fresh parsley Shaved Parmesan cheese (optional)

1. Cook pasta according to package directions, adding broccoli the last 3 minutes of cooking; drain.

2. Meanwhile, drain beans, reserving ¼ cup of the liquid. In a 12-inch skillet heat oil over medium-high. Add onions and salt; reduce heat to medium. Cook about 5 minutes or until tender, stirring occasionally.

3. Increase heat to high; stir in cooked pasta mixture, beans, the reserved bean liquid, the broth, and chili powder. Cook 2 minutes, stirring occasionally. Add shredded cheese and parsley. Cook and stir until cheese is melted. If desired, top each serving with shaved cheese.

PER SERVING *(1¾ cups each)* **CAL** 319, **FAT** 7 g (2 g sat. fat), **CHOL** 7 mg, **SODIUM** 455 mg, **CARB** 48 g (13 g fiber, 5 g sugars), **PRO** 18 g

Roasted Vegetable Pasta with Walnuts and Sage

36 g
CARB

SERVES	4
HANDS ON	20 min.
TOTAL	40 min.

Nonstick cooking spray
- 2 cups ½-inch pieces carrots
- 8 oz. Brussels sprouts, trimmed (halved if large)
- 2 tsp. olive oil
- ½ tsp. salt
- ¼ tsp. black pepper
- 1¼ cups dried multigrain penne pasta
- 1 15-oz. can no-salt-added fire-roasted diced tomatoes, undrained
- 2 tsp. snipped fresh sage
- 1 oz. reduced-fat cream cheese (neufchatel), softened
- ⅓ cup grated Parmesan cheese
- ¼ cup broken walnuts, toasted

1. Preheat oven to 400°F. Line a 15×10-inch baking pan with foil; coat foil with cooking spray. In a large bowl combine the next three ingredients (through oil), ¼ tsp. of the salt, and ⅛ tsp. of the pepper. Spread in prepared baking pan. Roast 20 to 25 minutes or until vegetables are tender and lightly browned.

2. Meanwhile, cook pasta according to package directions. Drain, reserving ½ cup cooking water. Keep pasta warm.

3. In a 10-inch skillet bring tomatoes, sage, and the remaining ¼ tsp. salt and ⅛ tsp. pepper to boiling; reduce heat. Simmer 10 minutes.

4. Reduce heat to low and whisk in cream cheese until smooth. Stir in roasted vegetables, pasta, and cheese; cook and stir just until cheese is melted. If needed, stir in enough reserved pasta cooking water to reach desired consistency. Top servings with walnuts and additional sage.

PER SERVING (1¼ cups each) **CAL** 296, **FAT** 12 g (3 g sat. fat), **CHOL** 11 mg, **SODIUM** 518 mg, **CARB** 36 g (7 g fiber, 8 g sugars), **PRO** 12 g

Roasted Vegetable Pasta with Walnuts and Sage

BAKED POTATO FIX-UPS

When you need a quick but filling meal on the cheap, look no further than the simple baked potato. Skip the butter and pile on lean meat and colorful, nutritious veggies.

HOW TO BAKE A POTATO: Preheat oven to 425°F. Scrub one 6-oz. russet (can also be labeled baking or Idaho) potato under cold water. Prick all over with a fork, wrap in foil, and bake about 40 minutes or until tender. Cool 15 minutes, remove foil, and slice open to add toppings. Eat the skin to maximize nutrients.

Cottage Cheese and Roasted Tomato Baked Potato

Preheat oven to 425°F. In a 2-qt. baking dish combine **½ cup cherry tomatoes** and **2 tsp. olive oil**. Roast about 20 minutes or until tomatoes burst open. Top a **6-oz. baked russet potato** with **¼ cup low-fat cottage cheese**, roasted tomatoes, and **1 tsp. snipped fresh chives**.

SERVES 1. **CAL** 304, **CARB** 42 g (5 g fiber, 5 g sugars)

Bacon and Avocado Baked Potato

Top a **6-oz. baked russet potato** with **2 slices lower-sodium bacon**, cooked and crumbled; **¼ of an avocado**, peeled, seeded, and diced; **2 Tbsp. Newman's Own salsa**; and **2 Tbsp. shredded reduced-fat Colby and Monterey Jack cheese**.

SERVES 1. **CAL** 322, **CARB** 43 g (7 g fiber, 3 g sugars)

Marinara Meat Sauce Baked Potato

In a skillet cook **2 oz. lean ground beef** and **⅓ cup sliced fresh mushrooms**, stirring occasionally. Drain; add **3 Tbsp. Prego Heart Smart Traditional Pasta Sauce** and heat through. Top a **6-oz. baked russet potato** with meat sauce and **1 Tbsp. grated Parmesan cheese**.

SERVES 1. **CAL** 291, **CARB** 43 g (5 g fiber, 6 g sugars)

Italian Zucchini Baked Potato

Coat a nonstick skillet with **nonstick cooking spray**. Cook **¼ cup chopped zucchini**; **¼ cup canned no-salt-added diced tomatoes, undrained**; and **½ tsp. Italian seasoning, crushed** over medium until zucchini is tender, about 8 minutes. Stir in **¼ cup shredded Italian-blend cheese**. Top a **6-oz. baked russet potato** with zucchini mixture.

SERVES 1. **CAL** 281, **CARB** 42 g (5 g fiber, 5 g sugars)

BBQ Turkey Baked Potato

In an 8-inch nonstick skillet combine **1 oz. cooked ground turkey breast**, **⅓ cup chopped red sweet pepper**, and **1 Tbsp. barbecue sauce**. Cook over medium 3 to 5 minutes or until heated through. Top a **6-oz. baked russet potato** with turkey mixture and **1 Tbsp. sliced red onion**.

SERVES 1. **CAL** 241, **CARB** 47 g (5 g fiber, 10 g sugars)

Ham and Broccoli Baked Potato

In a small bowl microwave **½ cup small broccoli florets** just until tender. Microwave **3 Tbsp. diced lower-sodium ham** until heated through. Top a **6-oz. baked russet potato** with the ham, broccoli, **1 Tbsp. plain fat-free Greek yogurt**, and **¼ cup finely shredded reduced-fat cheddar cheese**.

SERVES 1. **CAL** 299, **CARB** 41 g (5 g fiber, 4 g sugars)

Tomato and Egg Baked Potato

Top a **6-oz. baked russet potato** with **1 coarsely chopped hard-cooked egg**, **¼ cup diced tomato**, **¼ cup diced green sweet pepper**, **2 Tbsp. finely shredded reduced-fat cheddar cheese**, and **1 Tbsp. plain fat-free Greek yogurt**.

SERVES 1. **CAL** 306, **CARB** 42 g (5 g fiber, 5 g sugars)

2

FRESH
SALAD MEALS

A protein-rich salad loaded with vegetables makes a refreshing and

satisfying meal. Whether you're in the mood for a hot or cold salad,

you'll find choices that are grain-based, meat-topped, and full of

richly-flavored vegetables. All are a colorful feast for the eyes and a

delight for the taste buds.

Lemon-Lime Chicken, Kale, and Mango Salad

22g CARB | **SERVES** 4
HANDS ON 20 min.
TOTAL 30 min.

1 lemon
4 5-oz. skinless, boneless chicken breast halves
3 Tbsp. lime juice
½ tsp. kosher salt
¼ tsp. crushed red pepper
¼ tsp. black pepper

4 cups coarsely chopped kale leaves (about ½-inch pieces)
1½ tsp. canola oil
1 ripe medium mango
1 tsp. minced fresh ginger
⅛ tsp. black pepper
1 cup fresh blueberries
¼ cup hazelnuts, toasted and coarsely chopped

QUICK TIP A mango has a large flat seed in the center. To halve the fruit, be sure to cut down on both sides of the seed.

1. Remove ½ tsp. zest and squeeze 6 Tbsp. juice from lemon. Place chicken in a resealable plastic bag set in a shallow dish. For marinade, in a bowl combine 3 Tbsp. of the lemon juice, the lime juice, ¼ tsp. of the salt, the crushed red pepper, and the ¼ tsp. black pepper. Pour marinade over chicken. Seal bag; turn to coat chicken. Marinate in the refrigerator 15 minutes.

2. Meanwhile, place kale in an extra-large bowl. Drizzle with oil. Using clean hands, massage oil into kale.

3. Halve, seed, peel, and chop mango, reserving the juice. Set chopped mango aside. For dressing, in a bowl combine the reserved mango juice, lemon zest, the remaining 3 Tbsp. lemon juice, the remaining ¼ tsp. salt, the ginger, and the ⅛ tsp. black pepper.

4. Drain chicken, discarding marinade. Heat a grill pan over medium-high. Add chicken. Cook 8 to 10 minutes or until done (165°F), turning once. If chicken browns too quickly, reduce heat to medium. Slice chicken.

5. Add chopped mango, blueberries, and hazelnuts to kale in bowl. Drizzle with dressing; toss gently to coat. Top kale mixture with sliced chicken.

Tip If you can't find 5-oz. chicken breast halves, buy two larger breast halves (1¼ lb. total) and cut them in half horizontally to make four chicken breast portions.

Tip To toast nuts, spread in a shallow baking pan lined with parchment paper. Bake in a 350°F oven 5 to 10 minutes or until golden, shaking pan once or twice.

PER SERVING (1 chicken breast half + 1½ cups kale mixture each) CAL 311, FAT 11 g (1 g sat. fat), CHOL 91 mg, SODIUM 355 mg, CARB 22 g (4 g fiber, 13 g sugars), PRO 35 g

Chicken-Broccoli Salad with Buttermilk Dressing

Chicken-Broccoli Salad with Buttermilk Dressing

29 g CARB

SERVES 4
HANDS ON 20 min.
TOTAL 2 hr. 20 min.

- 3 cups packaged shredded broccoli slaw mix
- 2 cups coarsely chopped cooked chicken breast
- ½ cup dried cherries
- ⅓ cup thinly sliced celery
- ¼ cup finely chopped red onion
- ⅓ cup buttermilk
- ⅓ cup light mayonnaise
- 1 Tbsp. honey
- 1 Tbsp. cider vinegar
- 1 tsp. dry mustard
- ½ tsp. salt
- ⅛ tsp. black pepper
- 4 cups fresh baby spinach

1. In a large bowl combine the first five ingredients (through onion). In a small bowl whisk together the next seven ingredients (through pepper). Pour buttermilk mixture over broccoli mixture; toss gently to combine. Cover and chill at least 2 hours or up to 24 hours before serving.

2. Just before serving, add baby spinach and toss gently to combine.

PER SERVING (2 cups each) CAL 278, FAT 7 g (2 g sat. fat), CHOL 64 mg, SODIUM 585 mg, CARB 29 g (4 g fiber, 19 g sugars), PRO 26 g

Thai Chicken and Noodle Salad

39 g CARB

SERVES 1
TOTAL 20 min.

- 3 Tbsp. powdered peanut butter
- 2 Tbsp. water
- 3 Tbsp. unsweetened light coconut milk
- 1 Tbsp. lime juice
- 2 tsp. reduced-sodium soy sauce
- ¼ tsp. sriracha sauce
- 1 oz. dried whole grain spaghetti, broken in half, cooked, and drained
- ½ cup snow pea pods, trimmed and halved crosswise
- ⅓ cup chopped cooked chicken breast
- ¼ cup bite-size pieces red sweet pepper
- 1 tsp. snipped fresh cilantro
- 1 Tbsp. sliced green onion
- 1 Tbsp. chopped unsalted peanuts

1. In a medium bowl stir together powdered peanut butter and the water. Stir in the next four ingredients (through sriracha sauce) until smooth. Add the next five ingredients (through cilantro); toss to coat. Sprinkle with green onion and peanuts.

PER SERVING *(1¾ cups each)* **CAL** 388, **FAT** 12 g (3 g sat. fat), **CHOL** 48 mg, **SODIUM** 588 mg, **CARB** 39 g (9 g fiber, 8 g sugars), **PRO** 34 g

Thai Chicken and Noodle Salad

Spinach-Feta Rice Salad with Chicken Sausage

35 g CARB

SERVES 4
HANDS ON 25 min.
TOTAL 1 hr. 10 min.

- 1 12-oz. pkg. fully cooked roasted garlic or roasted pepper-asiago chicken sausages
- ¾ cup uncooked brown rice

2   **cups fresh spinach, sliced**
1   **cup chopped cucumber**
¾   **cup chopped red sweet**
    pepper
1   **recipe Garlic-Herb Vinaigrette**
¼   **cup crumbled reduced-fat feta**
    cheese (1 oz.)

1.   Cut sausages in half lengthwise.
Thinly slice sausage halves crosswise.

Cook rice according to package
directions, omitting any added salt
and adding the sausage the last
3 minutes of cooking. Let rice cool
about 15 minutes.
2.   Stir in spinach, cucumber, and
pepper. Drizzle with Garlic-Herb
Vinaigrette. Toss to coat. Sprinkle with
feta cheese.

Garlic-Herb Vinaigrette In a
screw-top jar combine ⅓ cup snipped
fresh parsley; 2 Tbsp. lemon juice;
1½ Tbsp. olive oil; 1 Tbsp. white wine
vinegar; 1 tsp. each mustard and
honey; and 1 clove garlic, minced.
Cover and shake well.

PER SERVING *(2 cups each)* **CAL** 357,
FAT 15 g (4 g sat. fat), **CHOL** 70 mg,
SODIUM 596 mg, **CARB** 35 g (3 g fiber,
6 g sugars), **PRO** 20 g

Bacon-Wrapped Turkey Meatball and Cabbage Salad

Bacon-Wrapped Turkey Meatball and Cabbage Salad

26 g CARB

SERVES 4
HANDS ON 25 min.
TOTAL 45 min.

¼ cup refrigerated or frozen egg product, thawed, or 1 egg, lightly beaten
¼ cup fat-free milk
¼ cup dry whole wheat bread crumbs
½ tsp. caraway seeds, crushed
12 oz. ground turkey breast
8 strips lower-sodium, less-fat bacon, halved crosswise
2 Tbsp. honey
2 tsp. Dijon-style mustard
½ tsp. cornstarch
⅓ cup cider vinegar
7 cups coarsely chopped green cabbage (1- to 2-inch pieces)
Nonstick olive oil cooking spray

2 medium carrots
⅓ cup reduced-fat blue cheese salad dressing
2 Tbsp. fat-free milk

1. Preheat oven to 375°F. Line a 15×10-inch baking pan with foil or parchment paper. In a large bowl combine the first four ingredients (through caraway seeds). Add turkey; mix well. Divide into 16 equal portions; shape into balls. Wrap each meatball with half a strip of bacon. Place bacon-wrapped meatballs, seam sides down, in prepared pan.

2. Bake meatballs 15 to 18 minutes or until bacon is cooked through and meatballs are no longer pink (165°F).

3. Meanwhile, in a small saucepan whisk together honey, mustard, and cornstarch until smooth. Whisk in vinegar. Cook and stir over medium until slightly thickened and bubbly.

Remove from heat. Brush over meatballs. Let meatballs cool slightly in the pan on a wire rack.

4. Preheat the broiler. Spread cabbage in a 15×10-inch baking pan. Lightly coat cabbage with cooking spray.

5. Broil cabbage 4 to 5 inches from the heat 4 to 5 minutes or until lightly browned and charred in places and lightly wilted, stirring once.

6. Peel the carrots. Use the peeler to make long thin strips of carrot.

7. To serve, top cabbage with carrot strips and meatballs. If desired, drizzle meatballs with additional glaze. In a small bowl stir together blue cheese dressing and the 2 Tbsp. milk until smooth. Drizzle over salads.

PER SERVING *(1 cup salad + 4 meatballs + 2 Tbsp. dressing)* **CAL** 285, **FAT** 6 g (2 g sat. fat), **CHOL** 41 mg, **SODIUM** 585 mg, **CARB** 26 g (5 g fiber, 16 g sugars), **PRO** 31 g

Strawberry-Turkey Salad with Creamy Curry Dressing

18 g CARB

SERVES 4
TOTAL 15 min.

2 cups chopped cooked turkey breast
1 recipe Creamy Curry Dressing
6 cups baby spinach
1 cup sliced strawberries
2 naval and/or Cara Cara oranges, peeled and sectioned
¼ cup chopped peanuts
2 green onions, sliced

1. In a bowl toss together the chopped turkey and dressing.

2. Arrange greens on a large serving platter. Top with turkey mixture, strawberries, and oranges. Sprinkle with peanuts and green onions.

Creamy Curry Dressing In a bowl whisk together 2 Tbsp. each plain fat-free Greek yogurt and light mayonnaise, 1 tsp. curry powder, ⅛ tsp. salt, and a dash black pepper. Stir in enough fat-free milk (2 to 3 Tbsp.) to reach desired consistency.

PER SERVING (2¼ cups each) CAL 241, FAT 8 g (1 g sat. fat), CHOL 51 mg, SODIUM 326 mg, CARB 18 g (6 g fiber, 9 g sugars), PRO 27 g

QUICK TIP To toast bread cubes, spread bread cubes in a 15×10-inch baking pan. Bake in a 350°F oven about 10 minutes or until golden, stirring once.

Steak and Chimichurri Salad

Steak and Chimichurri Salad

22 g
CARB

SERVES 4
HANDS ON 30 min.
TOTAL 45 min.

- 12 oz. beef flank steak
- ¼ tsp. salt
- ¼ tsp. black pepper
- 1 recipe Chimichurri Sauce
- 4 oz. whole grain baguette-style French bread, cut into ½-inch cubes, toasted
- 1½ cups cherry tomatoes, halved
- ½ cup very thinly sliced, quartered red onion
- 4 cups fresh arugula or baby mixed greens

1. Trim fat from steak. Score both sides of steak in a diamond pattern by making shallow diagonal cuts at 1-inch intervals. Sprinkle both sides of steak with salt and pepper. Let stand 5 minutes.
2. Meanwhile, make the Chimichurri Sauce.
3. Grill steak, covered, over medium heat 13 to 18 minutes or until meat reaches desired doneness (160°F for medium), turning once. Brush steak with 2 Tbsp. Chimichurri Sauce during the last 5 minutes of grilling.
4. In a large bowl combine bread cubes, tomatoes, onion, arugula, and remaining Chimichurri Sauce; toss until well coated.
5. Thinly slice steak across the grain. Top salad mixture with steak slices.

Chimichurri Sauce In a blender or food processor, combine ¾ cup each tightly packed fresh Italian parsley and fresh cilantro; ¼ cup lime juice; 2 Tbsp. red wine vinegar; 1 Tbsp. each olive oil and water; 3 cloves garlic, minced; and ¼ tsp. each crushed red pepper and salt. Cover and pulse until nearly smooth but still slightly chunky.

PER SERVING (1¾ cups each) **CAL** 284, **FAT** 12 g (4 g sat. fat), **CHOL** 49 mg, **SODIUM** 514 mg, **CARB** 22 g (2 g fiber, 3 g sugars), **PRO** 23 g

Buffalo-Spiced Steak Salads with Blue Cheese Dressing

Buffalo-Spiced Steak Salads with Blue Cheese Dressing

8 g
CARB

SERVES 4
HANDS ON 15 min.
TOTAL 30 min.

- 1 1-lb. beef flank steak
- 1 tsp. packed brown sugar*
- ½ tsp. kosher salt
- ½ tsp. garlic powder
- ½ tsp. paprika
- ½ tsp. chili powder
- ½ tsp. cayenne pepper
- ½ tsp. coarsely ground black pepper
- 1 5.3-oz. carton plain fat-free Greek yogurt
- 2 Tbsp. buttermilk
- 1 tsp. Buffalo wing sauce
- ½ tsp. Worcestershire sauce
- ¼ cup crumbled blue cheese (1 oz.)
- 1 stalk celery
- 1 medium carrot
- 6 cups mixed salad greens Celery leaves (optional)

1. Trim fat from meat. For rub, in a bowl stir together the next seven ingredients (through black pepper). Sprinkle mixture evenly over meat; rub in with your fingers. Let stand at room temperature 10 minutes.
2. Meanwhile, for dressing, in a bowl stir together yogurt, buttermilk, Buffalo wing sauce, and Worcestershire sauce. Stir in blue cheese. Cover and chill until ready to serve. Using a vegetable peeler, cut celery stalk and carrot lengthwise into thin ribbons.
3. Grill steak, covered, over medium heat 13 to 18 minutes or until meat reaches desired doneness (160°F for medium), turning once. Thinly slice steak across the grain.
4. Top mixed greens with celery and carrot ribbons and sliced steak. Serve with dressing and, if desired, garnish with celery leaves.

***Sugar Sub** Choose Splenda Brown Sugar Blend. Follow package directions to use 1 tsp. equivalent.

PER SERVING (3 oz. meat + 2 cups salad + about ¼ cup dressing each) **CAL** 255, **FAT** 10 g (5 g sat. fat), **CHOL** 86 mg, **SODIUM** 564 mg, **CARB** 8 g (2 g fiber, 5 g sugars), **PRO** 32 g

PER SERVING WITH SUB Same as above, except **CAL** 251, **CARB** 7 g (3 g sugars)

Steak Salad with Creamy Horseradish Dressing

22 g CARB

SERVES 4
HANDS ON 15 min.
TOTAL 1 hr.

- 8 oz. new potatoes, quartered
- 8 oz. fresh green beans, trimmed
- 1 small red onion, cut into ½-inch-thick wedges
- 1 Tbsp. olive oil
- ½ tsp. salt
- 2 8-oz. boneless beef top sirloin steaks, cut 1 inch thick
- ¼ tsp. cracked black pepper
  Nonstick cooking spray
- 6 cups torn Bibb lettuce or romaine lettuce
- 1 recipe Creamy Horseradish Dressing

1. Preheat oven to 425°F. Arrange potatoes, green beans, and onion wedges in a single layer in a shallow baking pan. Drizzle with olive oil and sprinkle with ¼ tsp. of the salt. Roast 25 to 30 minutes or until tender, stirring once.

2. Meanwhile, trim fat from steaks. Sprinkle steaks with remaining ¼ tsp. salt and the cracked black pepper. Coat a 10-inch skillet with cooking spray. Heat over medium-high until very hot. Add steaks. Reduce heat to medium and cook 15 to 20 minutes or until desired doneness (145°F for medium rare or 160°F for medium). Let stand 5 minutes. Slice steaks across the grain into ¼-inch-thick slices.

3. Arrange greens on a platter. Top with potato mixture. Arrange steak slices over potato mixture. Drizzle with horseradish dressing.

Creamy Horseradish Dressing In a small bowl combine one 5.3-oz. carton plain fat-free Greek yogurt, 1 Tbsp. each prepared horseradish and snipped fresh chives, 1 tsp. each honey and red wine vinegar, and a dash salt. Stir in enough of 3 to 4 Tbsp. milk to reach desired consistency.

PER SERVING *(2¼ cups salad + 3 oz. steak + 3 Tbsp. dressing each)* **CAL** 294, **FAT** 9 g (2 g sat. fat), **CHOL** 68 mg, **SODIUM** 450 mg, **CARB** 22 g (4 g fiber, 8 g sugars), **PRO** 33 g

Balsamic Pork and
Strawberry Salad

Balsamic Pork and Strawberry Salad

13g
CARB

SERVES 4
HANDS ON 15 min.
TOTAL 55 min.

- 1 1-lb. natural pork tenderloin
- ½ cup balsamic vinegar
- 2 Tbsp. Dijon-style mustard
- 1 Tbsp. olive oil
- ¼ tsp. salt
- ¼ tsp. black pepper
- 4 cups torn romaine lettuce
- 2 cups quartered fresh strawberries
- ½ cup shredded Manchego cheese (2 oz.)

1. Trim fat from meat. Place meat in a resealable plastic bag set in a shallow dish. For marinade, in a bowl whisk together balsamic vinegar and mustard. Set aside 3 Tbsp. of the marinade. Pour the remaining marinade over pork. Seal bag; turn to coat pork. Marinate in the refrigerator 15 minutes.

2. Preheat oven to 425°F. Line a shallow roasting pan with foil. Drain meat, discarding marinade. Place meat in the prepared roasting pan. Roast 25 to 30 minutes or until a thermometer inserted in meat registers 145°F. Remove from oven; let stand 3 minutes. Slice pork.

3. Meanwhile, for salad, in a large bowl whisk together the reserved 3 Tbsp. marinade, the oil, salt, and pepper. Add lettuce and strawberries; toss gently to coat.

4. Arrange salad on a serving platter; sprinkle with cheese. Arrange sliced pork on top of salad.

PER SERVING (3 oz. meat + 1½ cups salad each) **CAL** 278, **FAT** 12 g (5 g sat. fat), **CHOL** 88 mg, **SODIUM** 511 mg, **CARB** 13 g (2 g fiber, 9 g sugars), **PRO** 28 g

Delicata Squash Salad with Pork Medallions

19 g CARB

SERVES 4
HANDS ON 15 min.
TOTAL 30 min.

- 12 oz. pork tenderloin, cut into ½-inch slices
- ¼ tsp. salt
- ½ tsp. black pepper
- 1 Tbsp. olive oil
- 3 strips lower-sodium, less-fat bacon
- 1 lb. delicata squash, seeds removed and cut into 1-inch pieces
- ¾ cup unsweetened apple juice
- ¼ cup water
- 2 shallots, thinly sliced
- 3 Tbsp. cider vinegar
- 1 tsp. snipped fresh thyme or ¼ tsp. dried thyme, crushed
- 6 cups fresh baby spinach

1. Sprinkle pork with salt and ¼ tsp. of the pepper. In a 10-inch nonstick skillet cook pork in hot oil over medium-high about 5 minutes or until browned but still slightly pink in center, turning once. Remove from skillet; keep warm.
2. In the same skillet cook bacon over medium heat until crisp. Drain bacon on paper towels. Crumble bacon. Wipe skillet clean. Add squash, apple juice, the water, and the shallots to skillet. Bring to boiling; reduce heat. Cook, covered, 6 to 8 minutes or until squash is just tender.
3. Add vinegar, thyme, and the remaining ¼ tsp. pepper to skillet. Return pork and any accumulated juices to skillet; heat through. Serve over spinach. Sprinkle with bacon.

PER SERVING *(1 cup pork and squash mixture + 1½ cups spinach each)* **CAL** 226, **FAT** 6 g (1 g sat. fat), **CHOL** 58 mg, **SODIUM** 315 mg, **CARB** 19 g (4 g fiber, 5 g sugars), **PRO** 22 g

Delicata Squash Salad with Pork Medallions

Pork and Butternut Salad

Pork and Butternut Salad

31 g
CARB

SERVES 2
HANDS ON 25 min.
TOTAL 50 min.

1   Tbsp. balsamic vinegar
2   tsp. olive oil
¼   tsp. salt
¼   tsp. ground cinnamon
¼   tsp. black pepper
¾   cup ¾-inch pieces butternut squash
¼   cup chopped onion
1   8-oz. boneless pork loin chop, cut 1 inch thick and trimmed of fat
1   Tbsp. pure maple syrup
1   Tbsp. chopped pecans (optional)
3   cups mixed baby salad greens
¼   cup dried cranberries

1. Place a 9-inch cast-iron skillet in the oven. Preheat oven to 425°F.
2. Meanwhile, in a bowl whisk together the first five ingredients (through pepper). In another bowl toss squash and onion with 2 tsp. of the vinegar mixture. Carefully arrange squash mixture around edges of hot skillet. Roast 5 minutes.
3. Brush both sides of chop with 1 tsp. of the vinegar mixture. Place chop in center of hot skillet. Roast 18 to 20 minutes more or until squash is tender and browned, turning chop and stirring vegetables once.
4. Drizzle maple syrup over chop and vegetables. If using, sprinkle pecans over vegetables. Roast 1 to 2 minutes more or until a thermometer inserted in chop registers 145°F and pecans are toasted. Remove from oven and let stand 3 minutes. Thinly slice chop.
5. In a bowl toss together salad greens, cranberries, meat, vegetables, and the remaining vinegar mixture.

PER SERVING (2 cups each) **CAL** 306, **FAT** 9 g (2 g sat. fat), **CHOL** 75 mg, **SODIUM** 363 mg, **CARB** 31 g (4 g fiber, 19 g sugars), **PRO** 27 g

Cajun Ahi Tuna Salad

8g CARB

SERVES 2
TOTAL 20 min.

8 oz. fresh or frozen ahi tuna steaks, thawed
1 Tbsp. salt-free Cajun seasoning
  Nonstick cooking spray
¼ cup light ranch salad dressing
3 cups bite-size pieces romaine lettuce
¼ cup quartered cherry tomatoes
¼ cup chopped celery
¼ cup chopped green sweet pepper
¼ cup sliced green onions

1. Rinse tuna; pat dry. Sprinkle with 2 tsp. of the Cajun seasoning; rub in with your fingers.
2. Coat an 8-inch nonstick skillet with cooking spray; heat skillet over medium-high. Add tuna; cook about 4 minutes or until desired doneness, turning once.
3. In a medium bowl combine ranch dressing and the remaining 1 tsp. Cajun seasoning. Add lettuce; toss to coat.
4. To serve, break tuna into bite-size pieces. Top lettuce mixture with tuna and the remaining ingredients.

PER SERVING (2 cups each) **CAL** 233, **FAT** 8 g (1 g sat. fat), **CHOL** 49 mg, **SODIUM** 361 mg, **CARB** 8 g (3 g fiber, 4 g sugars), **PRO** 29 g

Cajun Ahi Tuna Salad

QUICK TIP Store pine nuts in an airtight container in the refrigerator or freezer to keep them fresh. If you like, substitute toasted sliced almonds for the pine nuts.

Peppered Shrimp and Green Bean Salad

34 g
CARB

SERVES 4
HANDS ON 25 min.
TOTAL 50 min.

- 12 oz. fingerling potatoes, halved lengthwise (quartered if large)
- 2 Tbsp. olive oil
- 1 lb. fresh green beans
- 1 lb. fresh or frozen peeled and deveined medium shrimp, thawed
- 1 tsp. olive oil
- ¼ cup thinly sliced shallots
- 4 cloves garlic, minced
- 2 Tbsp. sherry vinegar
- 2 Tbsp. honey
- 1 tsp. black pepper
- ½ tsp. salt
- 3 Tbsp. snipped fresh Italian parsley
- 2 Tbsp. pine nuts, toasted

1. Preheat oven to 400°F. Line a large shallow baking pan with nonstick foil. In a large bowl toss potatoes with 1 Tbsp. of the oil. Spread potatoes in the prepared pan. Roast 10 minutes.
2. In the same large bowl toss green beans with the remaining 1 Tbsp. oil. Add green beans to potatoes in pan. Roast about 15 minutes more or until vegetables are tender.
3. Meanwhile, rinse shrimp; pat dry. In a 10-inch skillet heat the 1 tsp. oil over medium. Add shallots and garlic; cook and stir 2 to 3 minutes or until shallots are tender. Add shrimp and the next four ingredients (through salt). Cook and stir 1 to 2 minutes more or until shrimp are opaque.
4. To serve, combine roasted vegetables and shrimp mixture. Sprinkle with parsley and pine nuts.

PER SERVING (2 cups each) **CAL** 335, **FAT** 12 g (2 g sat. fat), **CHOL** 183 mg, **SODIUM** 450 mg, **CARB** 34 g (6 g fiber, 14 g sugars), **PRO** 27 g

Indian-Spiced
Cauliflower and
Chickpea Salad

Indian-Spiced Cauliflower and Chickpea Salad

33 g
CARB

SERVES 2
HANDS ON 20 min.
TOTAL 40 min.

1 Tbsp. curry powder
1 Tbsp. olive oil
¼ tsp. salt
1½ cups cauliflower florets
1 cup canned no-salt-added garbanzo beans (chickpeas), rinsed and drained
¾ cup ½-inch carrot slices
¼ cup plain fat-free yogurt
1 Tbsp. lime juice
½ tsp. black pepper
½ tsp. grated fresh ginger or ¼ tsp. ground ginger
½ tsp. minced fresh jalapeño chile pepper (tip, *p. 64*) (optional)
1 to 2 Tbsp. fat-free milk (optional)
2 cups torn red-tipped leaf lettuce
1 cup packed fresh Italian parsley
¼ cup thinly sliced red onion

1. Preheat oven to 450°F. In a medium bowl combine curry powder, olive oil, and salt. Add the next three ingredients (through carrots); toss to coat. Spread mixture in a 15×10-inch baking pan. Roast 20 to 25 minutes or until vegetables are tender, stirring once.
2. Meanwhile, for dressing, in a small bowl stir together the next four ingredients (through ginger) and, if desired, jalapeño pepper. If needed, thin with milk to desired consistency.
3. In a large bowl combine roasted vegetables, lettuce, parsley, and onion. Top with dressing; toss to coat.

PER SERVING *(2½ cups each)* **CAL** 241, **FAT** 9 g (1 g sat. fat), **CHOL** 1 mg, **SODIUM** 405 mg, **CARB** 33 g (10 g fiber, 8 g sugars), **PRO** 11 g

Cauliflower-Watercress Salad with Dill-Shallot Dressing

Cauliflower-Watercress Salad with Dill-Shallot Dressing

18 g
CARB

SERVES 4
HANDS ON 35 min.
TOTAL 45 min.

- 1 bunch fresh asparagus (12 to 16 oz.), trimmed and cut into bite-size pieces
- ¼ cup water
- 6 cups small cauliflower florets (1½ lb.)
- 3 cups fresh baby spinach
- 3 cups fresh watercress, tough stems trimmed and coarsely chopped
- 1 medium orange or yellow sweet pepper, cut into thin bite-size strips
- 1 recipe Dill-Shallot Dressing
- 3 hard-cooked eggs, peeled and sliced
- ¼ cup thinly sliced, pitted ripe or Kalamata olives
- 1 oz. Parmesan cheese, shaved
  Cracked black pepper

1. Place asparagus in a 2-qt. casserole dish with 2 Tbsp. of the water. Microwave, covered, 2 to 4 minutes or until crisp-tender; drain. Transfer asparagus to a plate; let cool.
2. Meanwhile, place cauliflower in a food processor. Cover and pulse until cauliflower is evenly chopped into rice-size pieces. If necessary, process in batches. Add cauliflower to the same casserole dish with the remaining 2 Tbsp. water. Cover and microwave 6 to 9 minutes or until cauliflower is crisp-tender. Drain; cool cauliflower about 5 minutes.
3. To assemble salads, mix spinach and watercress with one-fourth of the Dill-Shallot Dressing. In a large bowl combine asparagus, cauliflower, sweet pepper, and the remaining Dill-Shallot Dressing. Spoon cauliflower mixture over greens. Top with sliced eggs, olives, cheese, and black pepper.

Dill-Shallot Dressing In a bowl combine ⅓ cup each finely chopped

Tabbouleh with Edamame and Feta

shallot and white wine vinegar. Cover and let stand at room temperature 15 minutes. Whisk in 2 Tbsp. mayonnaise, 2 tsp. snipped fresh dill weed or ½ tsp. dried dill weed, 1 Tbsp. olive oil, 1 tsp. Dijon-style mustard, and ⅛ tsp. salt until well combined.

Tip If desired, add 3 oz. thinly sliced, cooked boneless, skinless chicken breast to each salad.

PER SERVING (3½ cups salad + 3 Tbsp. dressing each) **CAL** 229, **FAT** 12 g (3 g sat. fat), **CHOL** 146 mg, **SODIUM** 485 mg, **CARB** 18 g (6 g fiber, 7 g sugars), **PRO** 14 g

Tabbouleh with Edamame and Feta

32 g
CARB

SERVES 6
HANDS ON 15 min.
TOTAL 30 min.

- 2½ cups water
- 1¼ cups bulgur
- ¼ cup lemon juice
- 3 Tbsp. purchased basil pesto
- 2 cups fresh or frozen edamame, thawed
- 2 cups cherry tomatoes, cut up
- ⅓ cup thinly sliced green onions
- 2 Tbsp. snipped fresh parsley
- ¼ tsp. black pepper
- ⅓ cup crumbled feta cheese
  Lemon wedges (optional)

1. In a medium saucepan bring the water to boiling; stir in bulgur. Return to boiling; reduce heat. Simmer, covered, about 15 minutes or until water is absorbed. Transfer to a large bowl.
2. In a small bowl whisk together lemon juice and pesto; drizzle over cooked bulgur. Let bulgur mixture cool to room temperature. Gently stir in the next five ingredients (through pepper). Sprinkle with feta. If desired, cover and refrigerate up to 4 hours before serving. If desired, garnish with additional snipped fresh parsley and/or lemon wedges.

PER SERVING (1 cup each) **CAL** 239, **FAT** 9 g (2 g sat. fat), **CHOL** 10 mg, **SODIUM** 176 mg, **CARB** 32 g (9 g fiber, 4 g sugars), **PRO** 12 g

Greens and Grain Italian Salad

35 g
CARB

SERVES 4
TOTAL 20 min.

- 6 cups mixed baby greens
- 1⅓ cups cooked and cooled pearled barley
- 1 15-oz. can no-salt-added red kidney beans or cannellini beans, rinsed and drained
- 1 cup coarsely shredded fresh basil
- 1 cup roma tomato wedges
- 1 recipe Balsamic Dressing
- 1 oz. shaved Parmesan cheese

1. Place greens on a platter. Arrange barley, beans, basil, and tomato wedges over greens. Drizzle with Balsamic Dressing and sprinkle with shaved Parmesan.

Balsamic Dressing In a bowl whisk together ¼ cup balsamic vinegar; 2 Tbsp. olive oil; 2 cloves garlic, minced; and ¼ tsp. each salt and black pepper.

PER SERVING *(2 ½ cups each)* **CAL** 267, **FAT** 10 g (2 g sat. fat), **CHOL** 5 mg, **SODIUM** 314 mg, **CARB** 35 g (8 g fiber, 5 g sugars), **PRO** 10 g

3

COMFORTING
SOUPS

Soups are the go-to when you want to enjoy hearty and healthful

goodness in a simple bowl. These full-meal recipes cover a

spectrum of flavors and styles. Here you'll find creamy chowders,

meat-loaded stews, and pasta- or grain-filled soups.

Chipotle Chicken and Corn Stew

QUICK TIP Chile peppers contain oils that can irritate your skin and eyes. Wear plastic or rubber gloves when working with them.

Chipotle Chicken and Corn Stew

25 g
CARB

SERVES 6
HANDS ON 25 min.
TOTAL 1 hr.

- 4 tsp. canola oil
- 1 lb. skinless, boneless chicken breast halves, cut into bite-size pieces
- 2 cups frozen whole kernel corn
- ½ of a 14.4-oz. pkg. frozen pepper and onion stir-fry vegetables
- 2 14.5-oz. cans reduced-sodium chicken broth
- 1 14.5-oz. can no-salt-added fire-roasted diced tomatoes, undrained
- 4 6-inch corn tortillas, torn into small pieces
- 2 tsp. salt-free Southwestern chipotle seasoning
- ¼ tsp. salt
- ¾ cup shredded reduced-fat mild cheddar cheese (3 oz.)
- ¼ cup thinly sliced green onions
- ¼ cup plain fat-free Greek yogurt (optional)
- 1 fresh jalapeño chile pepper, thinly sliced (optional)
  Lime wedges (optional)

1. In a 5- to 6-qt. Dutch oven heat 2 tsp. of the oil over medium. Add chicken; cook and stir until no longer pink. Remove from pan. Cover and chill until needed.

2. In Dutch oven heat remaining 2 tsp. oil over medium-high. Add corn and stir-fry vegetables; cook and stir 3 minutes. Stir in the next five ingredients (through salt). Bring to boiling; reduce heat. Simmer, covered, 30 minutes or until tortillas break down and broth is slightly thick. Stir in chicken. Simmer, uncovered, 5 minutes more.

3. Sprinkle servings with cheese and green onions. If desired, top individual servings with yogurt and jalapeño pepper and serve with lime wedges.

PER SERVING (1⅓ cups each) **CAL** 279, **FAT** 9 g (3 g sat. fat), **CHOL** 65 mg, **SODIUM** 577 mg, **CARB** 25 g (3 g fiber, 5 g sugars), **PRO** 26 g

Chicken Hummus Soup

Chicken Hummus Soup

26 g
CARB

SERVES 3
TOTAL 15 min.

Nonstick cooking spray
- 1 tsp. canola oil
- 6 oz. skinless, boneless chicken breast halves, cut into ½-inch pieces
- 2 cups no-salt-added chicken broth
- ½ cup hummus
- 1 cup ready-to-eat quinoa and brown rice blend
- ⅛ tsp. crushed red pepper
- 1 cup frozen sweet pepper and onion stir-fry vegetables

1. Coat a large saucepan with cooking spray. Pour oil into saucepan; heat over medium-high. Add chicken; cook and stir 4 to 5 minutes or until no longer pink.

2. In a bowl whisk together broth and hummus; add to chicken in saucepan. Stir in quinoa-rice blend and crushed red pepper.

3. Bring just to boiling over medium-high. Stir in frozen vegetables; reduce heat. Simmer 1 to 2 minutes or until vegetables are heated through.

PER SERVING (1⅓ cups each) **CAL** 262, **FAT** 9 g (1 g sat. fat), **CHOL** 36 mg, **SODIUM** 462 mg, **CARB** 26 g (3 g fiber, 1 g sugars), **PRO** 19 g

Chicken Paprikash Soup

Chicken Paprikash Soup

20 g CARB

SERVES 4
HANDS ON 10 min.
TOTAL 50 min.

- 1 cup chopped onion
- 2 cloves garlic, minced
- 1 Tbsp. olive oil
- 1 Tbsp. all-purpose flour
- 1 Tbsp. paprika
- ¼ tsp. kosher salt
- 1 cup canned crushed tomatoes
- 2 cups reduced-sodium chicken broth
- ¼ tsp. freshly cracked black pepper
- 1 lb. skinless, boneless chicken breast halves, cut into 2-inch pieces
- 1 8-oz. potato, peeled and cut into ½-inch cubes
- 6 Tbsp. light sour cream
  Fresh basil leaves (optional)

1. In a medium saucepan cook onion and garlic in hot oil over medium 3 to 4 minutes or until tender. Stir in flour, paprika, and salt. Cook and stir 1 minute more. Add tomatoes; stirring to scrape up any browned bits from bottom of saucepan. Simmer 3 to 4 minutes or until thickened. Add broth and bring to boiling.
2. Sprinkle pepper over chicken. Add chicken to broth mixture. Return to boiling; reduce heat. Simmer, covered, about 20 minutes or until chicken is no longer pink.
3. Using a slotted spoon, transfer chicken to a cutting board. Shred chicken using two forks.
4. Meanwhile, add the potatoes to the broth. Simmer, uncovered, 8 to 10 minutes or until tender. Stir in shredded chicken. Heat through.
5. Remove soup from the heat and stir in 4 Tbsp. of the sour cream. Top with remaining sour cream and, if desired, fresh basil leaves.

PER SERVING *(1¼ cups each)* **CAL** 271, **FAT** 9 g (2 g sat. fat), **CHOL** 79 mg, **SODIUM** 386 mg, **CARB** 20 g (3 g fiber, 2 g sugars), **PRO** 29 g

Lentil-Toasted Barley Soup
with Sausage

Lentil-Toasted Barley Soup with Sausage

31 g
CARB

SERVES 6
HANDS ON 35 min.
TOTAL 1 hr. 30 min.

1 Tbsp. olive oil
½ cup regular pearled barley
1 cup chopped onion
¾ cup chopped carrots
2 cloves garlic, minced
2 tsp. ground cumin
1 32-oz. carton reduced-sodium chicken broth
1 cup water
½ cup lentils, rinsed and drained
1 bay leaf

6 oz. cooked smoked chicken sausage with apple, halved lengthwise and sliced
4 cups fresh baby spinach

1. In a 4-qt. Dutch oven heat oil over medium. Add barley; cook and stir 3 to 4 minutes or until golden. Add the next three ingredients (through garlic); cook 10 minutes or just until vegetables are tender, stirring occasionally. Stir in cumin; cook and stir 30 seconds more.
2. Add the next four ingredients (through bay leaf). Bring to boiling; reduce heat. Simmer, covered, about 55 minutes or until barley and lentils

are tender. Stir in tomatoes and sausage; heat through. Remove and discard bay leaf. Add spinach, stirring until spinach begins to wilt. Serve immediately.

To Make Ahead Prepare as directed, except do not add spinach. Let soup cool. Store in the refrigerator up to 3 days. To reheat, bring soup to boiling. Add spinach and continue as directed.

PER SERVING (1⅓ cups each) **CAL** 235, **FAT** 7 g (2 g sat. fat), **CHOL** 28 mg, **SODIUM** 608 mg, **CARB** 31 g (6 g fiber, 3 g sugars), **PRO** 13 g

Beef Stroganoff Soup

Beef Stroganoff Soup

15 g
CARB

SERVES 6
HANDS ON 20 min.
TOTAL 50 min.

- 1 lb. boneless beef sirloin steak, trimmed and thinly sliced into bite-size strips
  Salt and black pepper
- 2 Tbsp. butter
- 3 cups sliced fresh button mushrooms
- 1 cup chopped onion
- 2 cloves garlic, minced
- 5 cups 50%-less-sodium beef broth
- 1 Tbsp. Worcestershire sauce
- 1 Tbsp. tomato paste
- 1½ cups dried egg noodles
- ½ cup sour cream
- 2 Tbsp. all-purpose flour
  Snipped fresh Italian parsley

1. Sprinkle meat with salt and pepper. In a 4-qt. Dutch oven melt butter over medium-high. Add meat, half at a time, and cook until browned. Remove from pan.

2. In same Dutch oven cook the mushrooms, onion, and garlic over medium 5 to 7 minutes or until onion is tender, stirring occasionally. Add the broth, Worcestershire sauce, and tomato paste. Bring to boiling. Stir in noodles; reduce heat. Boil gently, uncovered, 5 to 7 minutes or just until tender.

3. In a bowl combine sour cream and flour. Gradually stir in about 1 cup of the hot soup broth; return sour cream mixture to soup. Cook and stir until thickened and bubbly. Cook and stir 1 minute more. Stir in meat; heat though. Top individual servings with additional sour cream (if desired) and parsley.

PER SERVING *(1⅓ cups each)* **CAL** 248, **FAT** 11 g (6 g sat. fat), **CHOL** 72 mg, **SODIUM** 565 mg, **CARB** 15 g (1 g fiber, 4 g sugars), **PRO** 22 g

Dijon Beef Stew

Dijon Beef Stew

14 g
CARB

SERVES 6
HANDS ON 25 min.
SLOW COOK 8 hr. (low)

- 2 cups frozen small whole onions
- 2 cups packaged peeled fresh baby carrots
- 1 lb. beef stew meat, cut into 1-inch cubes and trimmed of fat
- 1 14.5-oz. can no-salt-added diced tomatoes, undrained
- 1 14.5-oz. can 50%-less-sodium beef broth
- 2 Tbsp. Dijon-style mustard
- 4 cloves garlic, minced
- 1 tsp. dried thyme, crushed
- ½ tsp. dried tarragon, crushed
- ¼ tsp. black pepper
  Fresh tarragon or parsley sprigs

1. Place onions and carrots in a 3½- or 4-qt. slow cooker. Top with stew meat. In a bowl stir together the next seven ingredients (through pepper). Pour over beef in cooker.

2. Cover and cook on low 8 to 10 hours or on high 4 to 5 hours. Garnish each serving with fresh tarragon sprigs.

PER SERVING *(1¼ cups each)* **CAL** 164, **FAT** 4 g (2 g sat. fat), **CHOL** 48 mg, **SODIUM** 370 mg, **CARB** 14 g (4 g fiber, 7 g sugars), **PRO** 19 g

**Pork and
Green Chile Stew**

Pacific Salmon Chowder

21 g
CARB

SERVES 6
HANDS ON 25 min.
TOTAL 50 min.

- 1 lb. fresh or frozen skinless salmon fillets
- 1 Tbsp. butter
- ½ cup chopped fennel bulb (leaves reserved)
- 2 cloves garlic, minced
- 1 32-oz. carton reduced-sodium chicken or vegetable broth
- 1¼ lb. Yukon gold potatoes, peeled (if desired) and cut into ½-inch pieces
- ¼ tsp. salt
- ¼ tsp. black pepper
- 1½ cups half-and-half
- 2 Tbsp. all-purpose flour
- 1 tsp. lemon zest

1. Thaw salmon, if frozen. Rinse salmon and pat dry. Cut into 1-inch pieces.
2. In a 4-qt. Dutch oven melt butter over medium. Add chopped fennel; cook 5 to 6 minutes or until tender, stirring occasionally. Add garlic; cook and stir 1 minute more.
3. Add the next four ingredients (through pepper). Bring to boiling; reduce heat. Simmer, uncovered, 10 minutes or until potatoes are tender.
4. In a bowl combine 1 cup of the half-and-half and the flour; stir into soup. Cook and stir until slightly thickened and bubbly. Stir in salmon. Return just to boiling; reduce heat. Simmer gently, uncovered, 3 to 5 minutes or until salmon flakes easily. Stir in remaining ½ cup half-and-half; heat through. Stir in lemon zest.
5. Coarsely snip fennel leaves and sprinkle over individual servings.

PER SERVING (1½ cups each) **CAL** 288, **FAT** 13 g (6 g sat. fat), **CHOL** 68 mg, **SODIUM** 551 mg, **CARB** 21 g (3 g fiber, 4 g sugars), **PRO** 21 g

Pork and Green Chile Stew

34 g
CARB

SERVES 6
HANDS ON 25 min.
SLOW COOK 7 hr. (low)

- 2 lb. boneless pork sirloin roast or shoulder roast
- 1 Tbsp. vegetable oil
- ½ cup chopped onion
- 4 cups peeled and cubed potatoes
- 3 cups water
- 1 15.25- or 15.5-oz. can hominy or whole kernel corn, drained
- 2 4-oz. cans diced green chile peppers, undrained
- 2 Tbsp. quick-cooking tapioca
- 1 tsp. garlic salt
- ½ tsp. ground cumin
- ½ tsp. ground ancho chile powder
- ½ tsp. black pepper
- ¼ tsp. dried oregano, crushed

1. Trim fat from meat. Cut meat into ½-inch pieces. In a 10-inch skillet cook half of the meat in hot oil over medium-high until brown. Using a slotted spoon, remove meat from skillet. Repeat with the remaining meat and the onion. Drain off fat. Transfer all of the meat and the onion to a 3½- or 4-qt. slow cooker. Stir in the remaining ingredients.
2. Cover and cook on low 7 to 8 hours or on high 4 to 5 hours.

PER SERVING (1⅔ cups each) **CAL** 347, **FAT** 7 g (2 g sat. fat), **CHOL** 89 mg, **SODIUM** 592 mg, **CARB** 34 g (4 g fiber, 3 g sugars), **PRO** 36 g

QUICK TIP Salmon offers a dose of heart-healthy omega-3s in this lemony chowder. Leave the potatoes unpeeled for extra nutrients and fiber.

Pacific Salmon Chowder

Charred Sweet Pepper Potato Chowder

Charred Sweet Pepper Potato Chowder

32 g
CARB

SERVES 4
HANDS ON 20 min.
TOTAL 35 min.

Nonstick cooking spray
3 cups chopped red sweet peppers
2 cups chopped yellow onions
1¾ cups chopped peeled russet potato
½ cup vegetable broth
2 cups milk
¼ tsp. salt
⅛ tsp. cayenne pepper
1 Tbsp. butter
¼ cup snipped fresh parsley
½ cup shredded sharp cheddar cheese (2 oz.) (optional)
¼ cup plain fat-free Greek yogurt (optional)
Crumbled crisp-cooked bacon (optional)

1. Coat a 4-qt. Dutch oven with cooking spray; heat over medium-high. Add sweet peppers; coat with cooking spray. Cook, uncovered, about 15 minutes or until charred, stirring frequently.
2. Add onions; cook 5 to 6 minutes more or until soft and golden brown, stirring occasionally. Stir in potatoes and broth. Bring to boiling, reduce heat. Simmer, covered, about 12 minutes or until potatoes are very tender. Coarsely mash pepper mixture. Stir in milk, salt, and cayenne pepper; heat through.
3. Remove from heat; stir in butter and parsley. If desired, top individual servings with cheese, yogurt, and/or bacon.

PER SERVING *(1¼ cups each)* **CAL** 209, **FAT** 6 g (3 g sat. fat), **CHOL** 17 mg, **SODIUM** 339 mg, **CARB** 32 g (5 g fiber, 15 g sugars), **PRO** 7 g

Broccoli Cheese Tortellini Soup

Broccoli Cheese Tortellini Soup

33 g
CARB

SERVES	6
HANDS ON	20 min.
TOTAL	40 min.

2 cups thinly sliced fresh mushrooms, such as button, cremini, or stemmed shiitake
½ cup chopped onion
3 cloves garlic, minced
1 Tbsp. olive oil
1½ cups reduced-sodium vegetable broth or stock
1 cup water
1 9-oz. pkg. refrigerated whole wheat three cheese tortellini
1 Tbsp. snipped fresh sage or 1 tsp. dried sage, crushed
1½ cups small fresh broccoli florets
1 cup fresh sugar snap peas, trimmed
3 cups low-fat (1%) milk
2 Tbsp. cornstarch
6 oz. reduced-fat cream cheese (neufchatel), cut into cubes and softened

1. In a 4-qt. Dutch oven cook mushrooms, onion, and garlic in hot oil over medium 5 minutes, stirring occasionally. Carefully add broth, water, tortellini, and dried sage (if using). Bring to boiling; reduce heat. Simmer, covered, 4 minutes.

2. Add broccoli; return to simmering. Cook, covered, 2 minutes. Add sugar snap peas; cook 2 to 3 minutes more or until tortellini are just tender.

3. In a bowl whisk together milk and cornstarch until smooth. Add all at once to the soup. Cook and stir until thickened and bubbly.

4. Place cream cheese in a bowl. Microwave about 30 seconds or until melted, stirring until smooth. Add melted cream cheese and fresh sage (if using) to the soup. Cook and stir until smooth.

PER SERVING *(1⅓ cups each)* **CAL** 321, **FAT** 15 g (6 g sat. fat), **CHOL** 53 mg, **SODIUM** 412 mg, **CARB** 33 g (5 g fiber, 11 g sugars), **PRO** 15 g

Curried Vegetable Soup with Quinoa and Tempeh

Curried Vegetable Soup with Quinoa and Tempeh

24 g
CARB

SERVES	6
HANDS ON	15 min.
TOTAL	40 min.

1 Tbsp. olive oil
1 8-oz. pkg. tempeh (fermented soybean cake), cut into ½-inch cubes
1 medium leek (white part only), halved lengthwise and thinly sliced (about ⅓ cup)
1 Tbsp. curry powder
1 32-oz. carton reduced-sodium vegetable broth
1 14.5-oz. can diced no-salt-added fire-roasted tomatoes, undrained
1 cup water
1½ cups kale or Swiss chard, stems removed and leaves coarsely chopped
½ cup quinoa, rinsed and drained
½ cup sliced carrot
½ cup frozen whole kernel corn
⅓ cup snipped fresh basil

1. In a 4-qt. Dutch oven heat 1½ tsp. of the oil over medium-high. Add tempeh; cook about 7 minutes or until golden, stirring occasionally. Remove from pan.

2. In the same pan heat the remaining 1½ tsp. oil over medium heat. Add leek; cook 2 to 4 minutes or until tender, stirring occasionally. Stir in curry powder. Add broth, tomatoes, and the water. Bring to boiling. Stir in kale, quinoa, and carrot. Return to boiling; reduce heat. Simmer, covered, 15 minutes. Stir in tempeh and corn. Simmer, covered, until quinoa is tender and tempeh is heated through. Stir in basil.

PER SERVING *(1⅓ cups each)* **CAL** 202, **FAT** 8 g (1 g sat. fat), **CHOL** 0 mg, **SODIUM** 362 mg, **CARB** 24 g (3 g fiber, 5 g sugars), **PRO** 11 g

Pork and Brown Rice Tomato Soup

Top **1 cup** heated tomato soup with **1 oz.** thinly sliced cooked pork tenderloin, **¼ cup** cooked brown rice, **1 Tbsp.** queso fresco, and **1 Tbsp.** snipped fresh cilantro.

SERVES 1. CAL 216, **CARB** 27 g (2 g fiber, 12 g sugars)

» TOMATO SOUP MIX-INS

For a quick and satisfying dish, stir any of these flavorful ingredient combos into your tomato soup. It's comfort in a bowl that brims with nutrition.

MOST TOMATO SOUPS are loaded with sodium. Look for a brand that has the lowest sodium content you can find or make your own.

Black Bean and Salsa Tomato Soup

Top **1 cup** heated tomato soup with **⅓ cup** no-salt-added black beans, **¼** of a chopped avocado, and **2 Tbsp.** Newman's Own Salsa.

SERVES 1. CAL 205, **CARB** 31 g (7 g fiber, 13 g sugars)

Yogurt and Basil Tomato Soup

Top **1 cup** heated tomato soup with **3 Tbsp.** plain fat-free Greek yogurt and **1 Tbsp.** snipped fresh basil.

SERVES 1. CAL 126, **CARB** 18 g (1 g fiber, 14 g sugars)

White Bean and Veggie Tomato Soup

Top **1 cup heated tomato soup** with **¼ cup no-salt-added cannellini beans, 2 Tbsp. cooked coarsely chopped broccoli florets,** and **2 Tbsp. cooked sliced carrots.**

SERVES 1. CAL 160, **CARB** 27 g (4 g fiber, 13 g sugars)

Orzo, Chicken, and Basil Tomato Soup

Top **1 cup heated tomato soup** with **2 Tbsp. cooked orzo, 1 oz. shredded cooked chicken breast,** and **1 tsp. basil pesto.**

SERVES 1. CAL 250, **CARB** 32 g (2 g fiber, 13 g sugars)

Beefy Tomato Soup

Top **1 cup heated tomato soup** with **1 oz. cooked lean ground beef, 1 Tbsp. chopped onion,** and **1 Tbsp. finely shredded reduced-fat cheddar cheese.**

SERVES 1. CAL 179, **CARB** 17 g (1 g fiber, 12 g sugars)

Tofu and Spinach Tomato Soup

Top **1 cup heated tomato soup** with **2 oz. diced firm tofu** and **½ cup fresh baby spinach.**

SERVES 1. CAL 146, **CARB** 18 g (2 g fiber, 12 g sugars)

4

PIZZAS &
SANDWICHES

These family favorites belong in your meal plan. The recipes shave

carbs with smart bread choices and serve up creative fillings.

Check out the economical make-ahead pizza crust that you can

keep in the freezer to use at a moment's notice to make individual

colorful, veggie-loaded pizzas.

Cheesy Turkey Sloppy Joes

Chicken Salad Panini

19 g
CARB

SERVES 4
TOTAL 25 min.

- ¼ cup light mayonnaise
- 1 Tbsp. balsamic vinegar
- 2 cloves garlic, minced
- 1½ cups chopped cooked chicken breast
- ⅓ cup finely chopped fennel bulb
- 8 slices very thinly sliced whole wheat bread
- ¾ cup arugula or spinach
- ¾ cup bottled roasted red peppers, drained and cut into thin strips
- 4 slices reduced-fat provolone cheese (3 oz. total)
  Olive oil nonstick cooking spray

1. In a medium bowl combine mayonnaise, vinegar, and garlic. Add chicken and fennel and stir until well combined.
2. Top four of the bread slices with chicken mixture, arugula, pepper strips, and cheese. Add the remaining bread slices.
3. Lightly coat an unheated panini griddle, covered indoor electric grill, or large nonstick skillet with nonstick cooking spray. Heat over medium or according to manufacturer's directions.
4. Place assembled sandwiches on griddle, grill, or skillet, adding in batches if necessary. If using griddle or grill, close lid and grill 2 to 3 minutes or until bread is toasted. (If using skillet, place a heavy saucepan or skillet on top of sandwiches. Cook 1 to 2 minutes or until bottoms are toasted. Carefully remove saucepan or top skillet [it may be hot]. Turn sandwiches; top again with the saucepan or skillet. Cook 1 to 2 minutes more or until bread is toasted.) Serve warm.

PER SERVING *(1 sandwich each)* **CAL** 285, **FAT** 12 g (442 g sat. fat), **CHOL** 62 mg, **SODIUM** 480 mg, **CARB** 19 g (3 g fiber, 3 g sugars), **PRO** 25 g

Cheesy Turkey Sloppy Joes

21 g
CARB

SERVES 6
HANDS ON 15 min.
TOTAL 45 min.

- 2 tsp. olive oil
- 1 cup chopped onion
- 1 lb. ground turkey breast
- ¾ cup chopped red sweet pepper
- 3 cloves garlic, minced
- 1 cup shredded reduced-fat cheddar cheese (4 oz.)
- ½ cup light mayonnaise
- 1 Tbsp. Worcestershire sauce
- 2 tsp. Dijon-style mustard
- 6 light whole wheat hamburger buns, split and toasted
  Leaf lettuce (optional)
  Sliced red onion (optional)
  Thinly sliced fresh jalapeño chile peppers (tip, *p. 64*) (optional)

1. In a 10-inch nonstick skillet heat oil over medium-low. Add chopped onion; cook, covered, 13 to 15 minutes or until onion is tender, stirring occasionally. Uncover; cook and stir over medium-high 3 to 5 minutes or until golden brown. Remove onion from skillet. In the same skillet cook turkey, sweet pepper, and garlic over medium until turkey is no longer pink. Drain off any fat.
2. Add cooked onion and the next four ingredients (through mustard) to turkey mixture. Cook and stir over medium-low just until cheese is melted.
3. If desired, line buns with lettuce and sliced red onion. Spoon turkey mixture onto buns. If desired, add jalapeño pepper slices to the sandwiches.

PER SERVING *(1 sandwich each)* **CAL** 295, **FAT** 12 g (4 g sat. fat), **CHOL** 53 mg, **SODIUM** 551 mg, **CARB** 21 g (7 g fiber, 6 g sugars), **PRO** 27 g

Chicken Salad Panini

Chicken Banh Mi Sandwiches

23g CARB | **SERVES** 4
HANDS ON 25 min.
TOTAL 4 hr. 40 min.

1 recipe Quick Pickled Veggies
4 5-oz. skinless, boneless chicken breast halves
1 Tbsp. rice vinegar
1 Tbsp. toasted sesame oil
2 tsp. reduced-sodium soy sauce
1 clove garlic, minced
½ tsp. ground ginger
½ tsp. crushed red pepper
3 Tbsp. light mayonnaise
1½ to 3 tsp. sriracha sauce
4 light whole grain hamburger buns, toasted
12 thin slices cucumber
¼ cup snipped fresh cilantro

1. Prepare Quick Pickled Veggies; chill as directed.

2. Meanwhile, place chicken in a resealable plastic bag set in a shallow dish. For marinade, in a bowl whisk together the next six ingredients (through crushed red pepper). Pour marinade over chicken. Seal bag; turn to coat chicken. Marinate in the refrigerator 2 to 4 hours, turning bag occasionally. Drain chicken, discarding marinade.

3. Grill chicken, covered, over medium heat 12 to 15 minutes or until chicken is done (165°F), turning once.

4. In a bowl combine mayonnaise and chili sauce. Drain Quick Pickled Veggies.

5. Spread cut sides of toasted buns with mayonnaise mixture. Top with cucumber slices, chicken, Quick Pickled Veggies, and cilantro. Add tops of buns.

Quick Pickled Veggies In a medium bowl combine ½ cup each bite-size carrot strips and bite-size daikon strips and 2 Tbsp. thinly sliced red onion. In a small bowl combine 2 Tbsp. rice vinegar, 1 Tbsp. sugar,* and ⅛ tsp. each salt, black pepper, and crushed red pepper. Microwave, covered, 30 seconds or until sugar is dissolved. Pour over vegetables; toss to coat. Cover and chill 4 to 24 hours, stirring occasionally.

*Sugar Sub Choose Splenda Sugar Blend. Follow package directions for 1 Tbsp. equivalent.

PER SERVING *(1 sandwich each)* **CAL** 335, **FAT** 11 g (2 g sat. fat), **CHOL** 93 mg, **SODIUM** 611 mg, **CARB** 23 g (7 g fiber, 8 g sugars), **PRO** 35 g

PER SERVING WITH SUB Same as above, except **CAL** 324 cal., **CARB** 20 g (5 g sugars)

Shredded Chicken Tacos

24 g
CARB

SERVES 8
HANDS ON 15 min.
SLOW COOK 5 hr. (low)

1 14.5-oz. can fire-roasted diced tomatoes, undrained
1 fresh jalapeño pepper, halved and stemmed (tip, *p. 64*)
3 cloves garlic, peeled
2 Tbsp. chili powder
1 Tbsp. ground cumin
½ tsp. salt
2 lb. skinless, boneless chicken thighs
16 6-inch corn or flour tortillas, warmed
   Guacamole, snipped fresh cilantro, and/or lime wedges (optional)

1. In a blender combine the first six ingredients (through salt); cover and blend until smooth. Pour tomato mixture into a 3½- or 4-qt. slow cooker. Add chicken thighs; stir to coat.

2. Cover and cook on low 5 to 6 hours or on high 2½ to 3 hours.

3. Remove chicken to a bowl. Shred chicken using two forks. Add enough sauce mixture from slow cooker to shredded chicken to moisten. Serve chicken in tortillas. If desired, top with guacamole, cilantro, and/or lime wedges.

PER SERVING *(2 tacos each)* **CAL** 256, **FAT** 6 g (1 g sat. fat), **CHOL** 106 mg, **SODIUM** 414 mg, **CARB** 24 g (4 g fiber, 4 g sugars), **PRO** 25 g

Shredded Chicken Tacos

≪ QUICK TIP Boneless, skinless chicken thighs are superior to breasts for slow cooking because they stay moist, are full of flavor, and shred easily.

Veggie-Filled
Hamburgers

Veggie-Filled Hamburgers

27 g
CARB

SERVES 4
HANDS ON 25 min.
TOTAL 35 min.

- 2 Tbsp. fat-free milk
- ½ cup finely shredded carrot
- ¼ cup thinly sliced green onions
- ¼ cup soft whole wheat bread crumbs
- 1 clove garlic, minced
- ¼ tsp. dried Italian seasoning, crushed
  Dash black pepper
- 12 oz. extra-lean ground beef (95% lean) or uncooked ground turkey breast or chicken breast
- 4 tsp. Dijon-style mustard
  Dash curry powder
- 4 lettuce leaves
- 4 to 8 slices tomato
- ½ cup sliced zucchini
- 4 whole wheat hamburger buns, split and toasted

1. In a bowl stir together the first seven ingredients (through pepper). Add the ground beef; mix well. Divide the mixture into four portions. Shape each portion into a ½-inch-thick patty.
2. Grill patties, covered, over medium heat 11 to 14 minutes or until done (160°F for beef or 165°F for turkey or chicken), turning once.
3. Meanwhile, for curry mustard, in a bowl stir together mustard and curry powder; spread on buns. Add patties, lettuce leaves, tomato, and zucchini to buns.

To Make Ahead Prepare as directed through Step 1. Place patties in a single layer in a freezer container. Cover and freeze up to 3 months. To serve, thaw in the refrigerator overnight.

PER SERVING (1 hamburger each) **CAL** 254, **FAT** 6 g (2 g sat. fat), **CHOL** 53 mg, **SODIUM** 359 mg, **CARB** 27 g (3 g fiber, 0 g sugars), **PRO** 24 g

Hot Dog with Cucumber-Avocado Slaw

Hot Dog with Cucumber-Avocado Slaw

32 g
CARB

SERVES 1
TOTAL 15 min.

- 1 uncured turkey hot dog
- ½ cup chopped, seeded cucumber
- ½ cup shredded cabbage with carrot (coleslaw mix)
- ¼ cup chopped red onion
- ¼ of an avocado, chopped
- 1 Tbsp. plain low-fat yogurt
- 1 Tbsp. sweet pickle relish
- 1 Tbsp. lime juice
- 1 reduced-calorie wheat hot dog bun

1. Place hot dog in a medium saucepan; add just enough hot tap water to cover the hot dog. Bring water to boiling; cook hot dog according to package directions.
2. Meanwhile, in a bowl toss together cucumber, coleslaw mix, onion, and avocado. For dressing, in a small bowl whisk together yogurt, pickle relish, and lime juice. Pour dressing over vegetable mixture; toss to coat.
3. Serve hot dog in bun; top with some of the slaw. Serve with the remaining slaw.

PER SERVING (1 hot dog in bun + 1¼ cups slaw) **CAL** 247, **FAT** 10 g (2 g sat. fat), **CHOL** 26 mg, **SODIUM** 537 mg, **CARB** 32 g (10 g fiber, 11 g sugars), **PRO** 12 g

Beef and Blue Wrap

Southwestern Steak Pizzas

29 g CARB

SERVES 6
HANDS ON 20 min.
TOTAL 45 min.

- 8 oz. beef flank steak
- ¾ tsp. salt
- ½ tsp. black pepper
- 2 medium avocados, halved, seeded, peeled, and mashed
- 2 tsp. lime juice
- 1 tsp. salt-free fiesta lime seasoning blend
- ¼ tsp. ground cumin
- 6 rounds Individual Pizza Crust (recipe, p. 87)
- ¾ cup shredded reduced-fat Mexican cheese blend (3 oz.)
- ½ of a 15-oz. can (¾ cup) no-salt-added black beans, rinsed and drained
- 1 cup grape tomatoes, quartered
- 2 Tbsp. light sour cream (optional)
  Fresh cilantro leaves

1. Trim fat from steak. Sprinkle steak with ½ tsp. of the salt and ¼ tsp. of the pepper. Grill steak, covered, over medium heat 17 to 21 minutes for medium (160°F), turning once. Remove from grill; let stand 5 minutes. Thinly slice steak diagonally across the grain.

2. Meanwhile, in a bowl combine the next four ingredients (through cumin) and the remaining ¼ tsp. salt and ¼ tsp. pepper.

3. Spread Individual Pizza Crust rounds with avocado mixture; sprinkle with cheese. Top with steak slices, black beans, and tomatoes. Grill pizzas, covered, over low heat 2 to 3 minutes or until heated through. Remove from grill. Top with sour cream (if desired) and cilantro.

PER SERVING (1 individual pizza each) **CAL** 291, **FAT** 12 g (3 g sat. fat), **CHOL** 32 mg, **SODIUM** 481 mg, **CARB** 29 g (7 g fiber, 1 g sugars), **PRO** 18 g

Beef and Blue Wrap

38 g CARB

SERVES 1
TOTAL 10 min.

- 1 8-inch low-carb, high-fiber whole wheat tortilla
- ½ cup fresh baby spinach
- ¼ cup fresh basil leaves
- 2 oz. lower-sodium deli-sliced roast beef
- 3 thin tomato slices
- ¼ cup cut-up sugar snap peas
- 1 Tbsp. crumbled reduced-fat blue cheese
- 1 tsp. light mayonnaise
- ½ tsp. balsamic vinegar
- ½ cup unsweetened applesauce

1. On the tortilla layer the next five ingredients (through sugar snap peas); sprinkle with blue cheese. In a bowl stir together mayonnaise and balsamic vinegar; drizzle over blue cheese. Roll up tortilla. Serve with applesauce.

To Tote Enclose wrap in plastic wrap. Carry in an insulated lunch box with a frozen ice pack.

PER SERVING (1 wrap) **CAL** 287, **FAT** 9 g (2 g sat. fat), **CHOL** 41 mg, **SODIUM** 535 mg, **CARB** 38 g (15 g fiber, 15 g sugars), **PRO** 27 g

Southwestern Steak Pizzas

Turkey, Apple, and Havarti Sandwiches

27 g
CARB

SERVES 2
TOTAL 10 min.

1 Tbsp. white wine vinegar
2 tsp. olive oil
½ tsp. Dijon-style mustard
 Dash black pepper
½ cup fresh baby spinach
⅔ cup thinly sliced apple
4 oz. roasted turkey breast, thinly sliced
2 ¾-oz. slices Havarti cheese
4 slices reduced-calorie whole wheat bread

1. For dressing, in a small screw-top jar combine vinegar, oil, mustard, and pepper; cover and shake well.
2. For sandwiches, layer spinach, apple, turkey, and cheese on two bread slices. Drizzle with dressing. Top with remaining bread slices.

PER SERVING (1 sandwich each) CAL 325, FAT 14 g (5 g sat. fat), CHOL 60 mg, SODIUM 460 mg, CARB 27 g (6 g fiber, 8 g sugars), PRO 27 g

> **QUICK TIP** To roast turkey, preheat oven to 400°F. In a 10-inch oven-going skillet heat 2 tsp. canola oil over medium-high. Add one 1-lb. turkey breast tenderloin; cook 3 minutes on one side or until golden. Turn turkey; transfer skillet to oven. Roast 15 to 20 minutes or until turkey is done (165°F). Transfer to a cutting board; cover with foil and let rest 10 minutes before slicing.

Farmstand Pizzas

Farmstand Pizzas

26 g
CARB

SERVES 6
HANDS ON 20 min.
TOTAL 30 min.

- ¾ cup fresh or frozen corn kernels, thawed
- ¾ cup 1-inch pieces fresh green beans
- 1 cup fresh baby arugula or baby kale
- ⅓ cup chopped red sweet pepper
- 1 Tbsp. lemon juice
- 2 tsp. olive oil
- ¼ tsp. salt
- ⅛ tsp. black pepper
- 6 rounds Individual Pizza Crust (recipe, *right*)
- 6 Tbsp. pizza sauce
- 1½ cups shredded part-skim mozzarella cheese (6 oz.)

1. In a covered medium saucepan cook corn in a small amount of boiling water 2 minutes. Add green beans; cook about 5 minutes more or until vegetables are crisp-tender; drain. Rinse with cold water; drain again.
2. In a medium bowl combine corn mixture, arugula, and sweet pepper. For vinaigrette, in a small screw-top jar combine lemon juice, oil, salt, and black pepper. Cover and shake well.
3. Spread Individual Pizza Crust rounds with pizza sauce; sprinkle with cheese. Grill pizzas, covered, over low heat 2 to 3 minutes or until heated and cheese is melted. Remove from grill. Top with vegetable mixture and drizzle with vinaigrette.

PER SERVING (1 individual pizza each) **CAL** 210, **FAT** 7 g (3 g sat. fat), **CHOL** 19 mg, **SODIUM** 356 mg, **CARB** 26 g (3 g fiber, 3 g sugars), **PRO** 11 g

Individual Pizza Crust

19 g
CARB

SERVES 12
HANDS ON 30 min.
TOTAL 40 min.

- 1½ cups whole wheat flour
- 1 cup all-purpose flour
- ¼ tsp. salt
- ¾ cup water

1. In a large bowl stir together whole wheat flour, ½ cup of the all-purpose flour, and the salt. Stir in the water to make a soft dough, adding additional water, 1 Tbsp. at a time, if necessary. Shape into a ball. Sprinkle some of the remaining ½ cup all-purpose flour on surface. Knead dough on surface until smooth, elastic, and slightly sticky. Cover; let stand 10 minutes.
2. Divide dough into 12 portions. Roll each portion into a ball. Press balls to flatten and coat lightly with more of the remaining flour. Using a rolling pin, roll dough into 6-inch rounds, using the remaining flour as necessary.
3. Heat a griddle or skillet over medium. Add a dough round; cook 30 seconds or until lightly browned. Turn over; cook 30 seconds more or until lightly browned and firm. Using a folded clean kitchen towel, evenly press rounds gently yet firmly. Repeat with remaining rounds.
4. Serve rounds immediately or let cool and store in an airtight container at room temperature up to 2 days or freeze up to 2 months.

To Grill Prepare as directed through Step 2. Grease grill rack. Grill dough rounds, in batches if necessary, covered, over medium heat 20 to 30 seconds or until lightly browned, rotating quarter turns for even cooking. Turn over; grill 20 to 30 seconds more or until lightly browned and puffed, rotating as necessary. Using a folded clean kitchen towel, evenly press the rounds gently yet firmly. The crusts will deflate as you press them.

PER SERVING (1 dough round each) **CAL** 89, **FAT** 0 g, **CHOL** 0 mg, **SODIUM** 49 mg, **CARB** 19 g (2 g fiber, 0 g sugars), **PRO** 3 g

Grilled Veggie and Goat Cheese Flatbreads

25 g
CARB

SERVES 4
HANDS ON 15 min.
TOTAL 30 min.

1 Tbsp. olive oil
½ tsp. salt
½ tsp. dried oregano, crushed
3 cups sliced fresh mushrooms
1 small zucchini, halved lengthwise and sliced ¼ inch thick (about 1 cup)
1 cup grape tomatoes, halved
1 medium onion, thinly sliced
¼ tsp. black pepper
4 rounds Individual Pizza Crust (recipe, *p. 87*)

Olive oil cooking spray
½ cup crumbled goat cheese (chèvre) (2 oz.)

1. In a small bowl combine 1½ tsp. of the oil, ¼ tsp. of the salt, and the oregano.
2. In a large bowl combine the next five ingredients (through pepper) and the remaining 1½ tsp. oil and ¼ tsp. salt; toss gently to coat. Place vegetables in a grill basket.
3. Grill vegetables in grill basket, covered, over medium heat about 10 minutes or until vegetables are tender, shaking and turning basket occasionally. Remove from grill.

4. Lightly coat one side of each Individual Pizza Crust round with cooking spray and place, coated sides down, on grill rack. Grill, covered, 2 to 3 minutes or until lightly browned and firm, rotating circles quarter turns as necessary for even cooking. Coat top sides of rounds with cooking spray, turn over, and brush with the oil-oregano mixture. Top with grilled vegetables and goat cheese. Grill, covered, 2 to 3 minutes more or until heated through.

PER SERVING *(1 flatbread each)* **CAL** 206, **FAT** 9 g (4 g sat. fat), **CHOL** 11 mg, **SODIUM** 421 mg, **CARB** 25 g (4 g fiber, 4 g sugars), **PRO** 9 g

Grilled Veggie and Goat Cheese Flatbreads

Tuna and Fennel
Sandwich

Tuna and Fennel Sandwich

31 g
CARB

SERVES 1

TOTAL 15 min.

1 2.6-oz. pouch low-sodium
  chunk light tuna in water

2 Tbsp. chopped green onion

1 Tbsp. light mayonnaise

2 tsp. tomato paste

2 very thin slices whole wheat
  bread

2 very thin slices fennel

½ cup fresh spinach

⅓ cup shredded carrot

½ cup raspberries

1. In a bowl combine tuna, green
onion, mayonnaise, and tomato paste;
spread on one slice of the bread. Top
with fennel, spinach, and carrot. Add
the remaining slice bread. Serve with
raspberries.

PER SERVING *(1 sandwich)* **CAL** 260,
FAT 8 g (1 g sat. fat), **CHOL** 38 mg,
SODIUM 510 mg, **CARB** 31 g (9 g fiber,
9 g sugars), **PRO** 20 g

Crunchy Tilapia Wraps
with Lemon-Dill Sauce

Crunchy Tilapia Wraps with Lemon-Dill Sauce

23 g **CARB**

SERVES 4
HANDS ON 20 min.
TOTAL 30 min.

- ½ cup plain fat-free Greek yogurt
- 2 Tbsp. lemon juice
- 1 tsp. dried dill
- ½ tsp. garlic salt
- ¼ tsp. white pepper
- 4 4- to 5-oz. fresh or frozen tilapia fillets
  Nonstick cooking spray
- ⅓ cup all-purpose flour
- 1 tsp. ground cumin
- ½ tsp. ground coriander
- ¼ tsp. salt
- 2 egg whites
- 1 cup panko bread crumbs
- 8 small butterhead (Boston or Bibb) lettuce leaves
  Thinly sliced cucumber
  Thinly sliced tomato, halved crosswise
  Thinly sliced red onion
- ¼ cup snipped fresh Italian parsley
  Lemon wedges (optional)

1. For sauce, in a bowl combine the first five ingredients (through white pepper). Cover and chill up to 24 hours.

2. Thaw fish, if frozen. Preheat oven to 425°F. Line a baking sheet with foil. Coat foil with cooking spray. Cut fish in half lengthwise. Rinse fish; pat dry with paper towels.

3. In a shallow dish stir together flour, cumin, coriander, and salt. In a second shallow dish lightly beat egg whites. Place panko in a third shallow dish.

Dip fish into flour mixture, then into egg whites. Coat with panko, pressing to adhere. Place on the prepared baking sheet. Lightly coat fish with cooking spray.

4. Bake 10 to 12 minutes or until fish flakes easily, turning once halfway through baking.

5. Divide fish among lettuce leaves. Top with cucumber, tomato, and red onion. Spoon some of the sauce over fish and vegetables; sprinkle with parsley. If desired, roll or wrap lettuce around filling. Serve with lemon wedges (if desired) and the remaining sauce.

PER SERVING (2 wraps each) **CAL** 241, **FAT** 3 g (1 g sat. fat), **CHOL** 56 mg, **SODIUM** 414 mg, **CARB** 23 g (1 g fiber, 3 g sugars), **PRO** 31 g

Shrimp Salad Sandwiches

32 g
CARB

SERVES 4
HANDS ON 20 min.
TOTAL 25 min.

- 1 lemon
- ¼ of a bunch fresh Italian parsley
- 8 oz. fresh or frozen peeled and deveined medium shrimp, thawed
- 1 medium mango, halved, seeded, peeled, and chopped
- ½ cup finely chopped celery
- ¼ cup chopped green onions
- ¼ cup plain fat-free Greek yogurt
- 1½ tsp. Dijon-style mustard
- ⅛ tsp. salt
- ⅛ tsp. black pepper
- 4 reduced-calorie whole wheat hamburger buns, split and toasted
  Lettuce leaves (optional)

1. Bring a large pot of water to boiling. Squeeze 1 tsp. juice from lemon; set aside. Squeeze the remaining juice into the boiling water; add lemon rinds. Remove leaves from parsley, reserving leaves and stems separately. Finely snip 2 Tbsp. of the leaves; set aside. Using 100%-cotton string, tie parsley stems into a bundle and add to the boiling water. Add shrimp.

2. Boil 1 to 2 minutes or just until shrimp are opaque. Using a slotted spoon, immediately transfer shrimp to a bowl of ice water to stop cooking. Drain and coarsely chop shrimp.

3. In a large bowl combine the reserved 1 tsp. lemon juice and 2 Tbsp. snipped parsley, the shrimp, and the next seven ingredients (through pepper). Serve shrimp mixture in toasted buns with lettuce (if desired).

PER SERVING *(1 sandwich each)* **CAL** 215, **FAT** 3 g (1 g sat. fat), **CHOL** 91 mg, **SODIUM** 419 mg, **CARB** 32 g (1 g fiber, 8 g sugars), **PRO** 18 g

Shrimp Salad
Sandwiches

Salmon Burgers with Coleslaw and Roasted Carrots

46 g CARB

SERVES 6
HANDS ON 40 min.
TOTAL 1 hr. 10 min.

3 cups packaged shredded cabbage with carrot (coleslaw mix)
¼ cup plain fat-free Greek yogurt
2 tsp. sugar*
2 tsp. red wine vinegar
½ tsp. celery seeds
¼ tsp. salt

2 lb. carrots, halved crosswise and cut lengthwise into sticks
1 Tbsp. olive oil
¼ tsp. black pepper
1 14.75-oz. can pink salmon, drained, flaked, skin and bones removed
¾ cup panko bread crumbs
½ cup finely chopped red sweet pepper
½ cup thinly sliced green onions
2 eggs, lightly beaten
Nonstick cooking spray
6 multigrain thin sandwich rolls, toasted

1. Preheat oven to 425°F. In a medium bowl combine the first six ingredients (through salt). Stir well to combine. Cover and refrigerate until needed.
2. Line a 15×10-inch baking pan with foil. Place carrots on baking pan. Drizzle with oil and sprinkle with black pepper. Stir to coat. Bake 25 to 30 minutes or until browned and tender.
3. In a large bowl combine the next five ingredients (through eggs). Shape into six 4-inch patties (about ⅓ cup each).
4. Coat a 12-inch nonstick skillet with cooking spray; heat over medium. Add patties; cook 4 to 5 minutes or until browned. Coat patty tops with cooking spray; turn. Cook 4 to 5 minutes more or until browned and cooked through (160°F). Place patties on sandwich rolls with coleslaw. If desired, top with additional sliced green onions. Serve with roasted carrots.

*Sugar Sub We do not recommend a sugar sub for this recipe.

PER SERVING (1 burger + ⅓ cup coleslaw + ½ cup carrots each) CAL 310, FAT 7 g (1 g sat. fat), CHOL 98 mg, SODIUM 581 mg, CARB 46 g (10 g fiber, 12 g sugars), PRO 20 g

Chipotle Ranch Egg Salad Wraps

Chipotle Ranch Egg Salad Wraps

25 g CARB | SERVES 2
| TOTAL 20 min.

2 hard-cooked eggs, peeled
¼ of a medium avocado, peeled and seeded
⅓ cup finely chopped green sweet pepper
1 green onion, thinly sliced
2 Tbsp. light ranch or light fiesta ranch salad dressing
1 Tbsp. lime juice
⅛ tsp. salt
Dash to ⅛ tsp. ground chipotle chile pepper
2 8-inch low-carbohydrate whole wheat tortillas
2 romaine lettuce leaves

1. In a bowl coarsely mash eggs and avocado until coarsely mashed. Add the next six ingredients (through chipotle pepper); stir to combine.
2. Lay tortillas on a flat work surface. Lay lettuce leaves on top of tortillas. Spoon egg mixture on bottom third of tortillas. Fold in sides of tortillas and roll up. Cut in half just before serving.

To Tote Leave wraps whole. Wrap individually in plastic wrap. Place wraps in insulated lunch boxes. Add cooler packs to lunch boxes or store lunch boxes in the refrigerator. Eat wraps within 5 hours.

PER SERVING (1 wrap each) CAL 256, FAT 13 g (3 g sat. fat), CHOL 189 mg, SODIUM 476 mg, CARB 25 g (5 g fiber, 4 g sugars), PRO 10 g

FLATBREAD FINESSING

Think of skinny, plain-Jane flatbreads as a base for amped-up toppings—plump veggies, tasty sauces, and gooey cheese. Use our mini recipes for inspiration to make a healthful main dish.

CHECK THE NUTRITION LABEL on thin pizza-crust flatbreads to select the one with the lowest carbs and fat. Use ½ of a flatbread and follow package directions to bake. For these recipes, top a prebaked flatbread, then bake again just a few minutes.

Chicken and Kale Flatbread

In a nonstick skillet saute **1 cup coarsely chopped kale** and **½ cup sliced red onion** in **1 tsp. olive oil** until softened. Top **½ of a flatbread** with **3 Tbsp. sliced cooked chicken breast**, kale, onion, and **¼ cup shredded part-skim mozzarella cheese**. Bake 4 minutes or until cheese is melted.

SERVES 1. CAL 283, **CARB** 25 g (5 g fiber, 6 g sugars)

Chicken Alfredo Flatbread

Cook **1 cup thinly sliced onion** in **1 tsp. olive oil** until golden and caramelized. Spread **2 Tbsp. light Alfredo sauce** onto **½ of a flatbread**. Top with **⅓ of a chicken and apple sausage, thinly sliced**, and onion slices. Bake 4 minutes. Top with **½ cup arugula**.

SERVES 1. CAL 249, **CARB** 29 g (4 g fiber, 9 g sugars)

Sweet Potato, Grape, and Feta Flatbread

Brush **1½ tsp. olive oil** onto **½ of a flatbread**. Top with **⅓ cup grilled sweet potato slices** and **¼ cup roasted halved grapes**. Bake 4 minutes. Top with **2 Tbsp. crumbled reduced-fat feta cheese**.

SERVES 1. CAL 219, **CARB** 27 g (3 g fiber, 9 g sugars)

BBQ Turkey Pineapple Flatbread

Spread **1 Tbsp. barbecue sauce** onto **½ of a flatbread**. Top with **3 Tbsp. shredded cooked turkey breast**, **¼ cup chopped pineapple**, **½ of a thinly sliced jalapeño pepper (tip, *p. 64*)**, and **¼ cup shredded part-skim mozzarella cheese**. Bake 4 minutes.

SERVES 1. CAL 219, **CARB** 24 g (2 g fiber, 11 g sugars)

Thai Peanut Chicken Flatbread

Spread **4 tsp. Thai peanut sauce** over **½ of a flatbread**. Top with **3 Tbsp. shredded cooked chicken breast** and **¼ cup shredded carrots**. Bake 4 minutes. Top with **1 Tbsp. thinly sliced green onion** and **1 Tbsp. coarsely chopped salted peanuts**.

SERVES 1. CAL 255, **CARB** 23 g (3 g fiber, 8 g sugars)

Mexican Flatbread

Spread **2 Tbsp. lower-sodium salsa** over **½ of a flatbread**. Top with **⅓ cup no-salt-added pinto beans, rinsed, drained, and slightly mashed**; **2 Tbsp. sliced black olives**; and **2 Tbsp. shredded Monterey Jack cheese**. Bake 4 minutes. Top with **1 Tbsp. sliced green onion**.

SERVES 1. CAL 220, **CARB** 27 g (6 g fiber, 2 g sugars)

Spinach and Egg Flatbread

Spread **2 Tbsp. pizza sauce** over **½ of a flatbread**. Top with **1 cup baby spinach** and **¼ cup coarsely chopped yellow sweet pepper**. Bake 4 minutes. Top with **1 soft-cooked egg**. Sprinkle with **black pepper**.

SERVES 1. CAL 167, **CARB** 17 g (3 g fiber, 4 g sugars)

5

SIMPLE SALADS &
SIDE DISHES

Choose from an exciting variety of starchy and nonstarchy

vegetables and grains to round out your meal plan and fill your

plate in a healthful way. These easy recipes check all the boxes for

low-calorie, tasty, nutritious, colorful meal accompaniments.

Flageolet Bean Salad with
Pesto and Feta Cheese

Flageolet Bean Salad with Pesto and Feta Cheese

12 g CARB

SERVES 8
HANDS ON 20 min.
TOTAL 3 hr.

- ¾ cup dried flageolet beans or navy beans (5 oz.)
- 6 cups cold water
- 2 stalks celery, halved crosswise
- 2 green onions, halved crosswise
- 2 sprigs fresh parsley
- 1 sprig fresh mint
- ½ cup packed fresh mint leaves
- ½ cup packed fresh parsley leaves
- 3 Tbsp. olive oil
- 2 Tbsp. crumbled feta cheese
- 1 tsp. lemon juice
- 1 small clove garlic
- ¼ tsp. kosher salt
  Dash black pepper
- 1 cup sliced celery
- 2 Tbsp. sliced green onion
- ⅛ tsp. kosher salt
- 1 Tbsp. snipped fresh mint
- 1 tsp. snipped fresh parsley

1. Rinse beans; drain. In a medium saucepan combine beans and 3 cups of the water. Bring to boiling; reduce heat. Simmer, uncovered, 2 minutes. Remove from heat. Cover and let stand 1 hour. (Or place beans in water in saucepan. Cover and soak in a cool place overnight.) Drain and rinse beans.

2. Return beans to saucepan. Stir in the remaining 3 cups water, the halved celery, halved green onions, 2 sprigs parsley, and 1 sprig mint. Bring to boiling; reduce heat. Simmer, covered, about 45 minutes or until beans are tender, stirring occasionally. Remove and discard vegetables and herbs. Drain beans, reserving 2 Tbsp. of the cooking liquid. Spread beans in a shallow dish; cover and chill at least 1 hour.

3. Meanwhile, for pesto, in a blender or food processor combine the ½ cup mint, ½ cup parsley, the oil, 1 Tbsp. of the feta cheese, and the next four ingredients (through pepper). Cover and blend or process until smooth, adding enough of the reserved cooking liquid if needed to reach desired consistency.

4. In a bowl combine beans, pesto, the sliced celery, sliced green onion, and the ⅛ tsp. salt. Top with the remaining 1 Tbsp. feta cheese and the snipped mint and parsley.

PER SERVING *(½ cup each)* **CAL** 116, **FAT** 6 g (1 g sat. fat), **CHOL** 2 mg, **SODIUM** 144 mg, **CARB** 12 g (4 g fiber, 1 g sugars), **PRO** 5 g

Black Bean and Corn Salad

28 g CARB

SERVES 4
TOTAL 15 min.

- 1 cup canned reduced-sodium black beans, rinsed and drained
- 1 cup frozen whole kernel corn, thawed
- 1 cup chopped avocado
- ½ cup chopped red onion
- ½ cup snipped fresh cilantro
- ¼ cup lime juice

1. In a bowl toss together all ingredients. Serve immediately.

PER SERVING *(1 cup each)* **CAL** 197, **FAT** 9 g (1 g sat. fat), **CHOL** 0 mg, **SODIUM** 129 mg, **CARB** 28 g (8 g fiber, 3 g sugars), **PRO** 6 g

Black Bean and Corn Salad

Baked Chicken Taquitos
recipe, *p. 9*

Kale and Raisins Salad

13 g CARB

SERVES 8
HANDS ON 20 min.
TOTAL 4 hr. 20 min.

- ⅓ cup buttermilk or plain fat-free Greek yogurt
- 2 Tbsp. light mayonnaise
- 1 Tbsp. sugar*
- 1 Tbsp. cider vinegar
- ¼ tsp. salt
  Dash cayenne pepper
- 5 oz. fresh kale, stemmed and torn into 1-inch pieces (about 8 cups)
- ½ cup slivered red onion
- ½ cup raisins or chopped pitted dried plums (prunes)
- ¼ cup sunflower kernels
- 2 slices lower-sodium, less-fat bacon, cooked and crumbled

1. In a large bowl combine the first six ingredients (through cayenne pepper). Add kale, onion, and raisins; toss to coat. Cover and chill 4 to 24 hours.
2. Before serving, add sunflower kernels and bacon to kale mixture; toss to combine.

***Sugar Sub** Choose Splenda Sugar Blend. Follow package directions to use 1 Tbsp. equivalent.

Tip To bake bacon, place slices side by side on a rack in a foil-lined shallow baking pan with sides. Bake in a 400°F oven 18 to 21 minutes or until bacon is crisp-cooked. Drain well on paper towels.

PER SERVING *(¾ cup each)* **CAL** 93, **FAT** 4 g (1 g sat. fat), **CHOL** 3 mg, **SODIUM** 159 mg, **CARB** 13 g (2 g fiber, 9 g sugars), **PRO** 3 g

PER SERVING WITH SUB Same as above, except **CAL** 103, **CARB** 16 g (8 g sugars)

Kale and Raisins Salad

Summer Garden Salad with Basil Vinaigrette

14 g CARB

SERVES 8
HANDS ON 30 min.
TOTAL 1 hr.

- ½ cup packed fresh basil leaves
- 1 Tbsp. sugar*
- ¼ tsp. salt
- 3 Tbsp. white wine vinegar
- 1 tsp. Dijon-style mustard
- 3 Tbsp. olive oil
- 4 ears of corn, husks and silks removed
- 1 cup fresh green beans, trimmed (if desired) and halved
- 1¼ cups chopped cucumber
- 1 cup cherry tomatoes, halved
- ½ cup chopped red sweet pepper
- 6 Tbsp. thinly sliced green onions

1. For vinaigrette, in a food processor or blender combine basil, sugar, and salt. Cover and process or blend until basil is finely chopped, stopping to scrape sides as necessary. Add vinegar and Dijon mustard; cover and process until combined. With processor running, slowly add oil in a steady stream until mixture is smooth.
2. Cut corn kernels from cobs; discard cobs. In a large saucepan cook corn and green beans in a large amount of boiling water about 5 minutes or until crisp-tender; drain. Rinse with cold water to cool; drain again.
3. In a large bowl combine corn and beans and the remaining ingredients. Pour vinaigrette over vegetables; toss to coat. Let stand at room temperature 30 minutes before serving.

***Sugar Sub** Choose Splenda Sugar Blend. Follow package directions to use 1 Tbsp. equivalent.

PER SERVING *(¾ cup each)* **CAL** 109, **FAT** 6 g (1 g sat. fat), **CHOL** 0 mg, **SODIUM** 98 mg, **CARB** 14 g (2 g fiber, 6 g sugars), **PRO** 2 g

PER SERVING WITH SUB Same as above, except **CAL** 104, **CARB** 12 g (5 g sugars)

**Summer Garden Salad
with Basil Vinaigrette**

Barley Waldorf Salad

23 g CARB

SERVES 8
HANDS ON 20 min.
TOTAL 1 hr.

- ¾ cup regular pearled barley or quinoa
- 3¾ cups water
- ½ tsp. salt
- 1 lemon
- ¼ cup plain low-fat yogurt
- 3 Tbsp. light mayonnaise
- ¼ tsp. sugar
- 1½ cups seedless red and/or green grapes, halved
- ⅔ cup coarsely chopped apple
- ½ cup sliced celery
- 8 butterhead (Boston or Bibb) lettuce leaves
- ¼ cup coarsely chopped walnuts, toasted
  Coarsely shredded lemon zest (optional)

1. In a large saucepan toast barley over medium-low 4 to 5 minutes or until golden brown, stirring occasionally. Add the water and ¼ tsp. of the salt. Bring to boiling; reduce heat. Simmer, covered, about 40 minutes or until tender (simmer about 15 minutes for quinoa). Drain; rinse with cold water until cool and drain again.

2. Meanwhile, remove ¼ tsp. zest and squeeze 1 Tbsp. juice from lemon. In a large bowl combine zest, juice, yogurt, mayonnaise, sugar, and the remaining ½ tsp. salt. Stir in cooked barley, grapes, apple, and celery.

3. To serve, spoon barley mixture onto lettuce leaves. Sprinkle with walnuts. If desired, top with coarsely shredded lemon zest.

PER SERVING (¾ cup each) **CAL** 141, **FAT** 5 g (1 g sat. fat), **CHOL** 2 mg, **SODIUM** 197 mg, **CARB** 23 g (4 g fiber, 7 g sugars), **PRO** 3 g

Smashed Potatoes

9g
CARB

SERVES	12
HANDS ON	20 min.
TOTAL	1 hr. 20 min.

- 12 to 16 small red potatoes (1½ to 2 inches in diameter; 1½ to 2 lb. total)
- ¾ tsp. salt
- ¼ cup olive oil
- ½ tsp. black pepper
- ½ cup finely shredded Parmesan cheese
- 2 Tbsp. snipped fresh Italian parsley

1. Place potatoes in a large saucepan and cover with at least 1 inch of water. Add ½ tsp. of the salt. Bring to boiling; reduce heat. Simmer, covered, 25 to 30 minutes or until potatoes are very tender; drain.

2. Preheat oven to 450°F. Transfer potatoes to a foil-lined 15×10-inch baking pan. Let cool 10 minutes. Using a potato masher or the palm of your hand (being careful not to burn your hand), lightly press down on each potato to smash to about ½-inch thickness, keeping each potato in one piece.

3. Brush half of the olive oil on potatoes. Sprinkle ¼ tsp. of the pepper on potatoes. Bake 10 to 15 minutes or until bottoms are lightly browned and crisp. Turn potatoes; brush with the remaining olive oil and sprinkle with the remaining ¼ tsp. each salt and pepper. Bake for 10 to 15 minutes more or until potatoes are lightly browned and crisp. In a bowl combine cheese and parsley. Sprinkle on potatoes. Bake 2 to 3 minutes more or until cheese melts.

PER SERVING (1 potato each) **CAL** 94, **FAT** 5 g (1 g sat. fat), **CHOL** 2 mg, **SODIUM** 188 mg, **CARB** 9 g (1 g fiber, 1 g sugars), **PRO** 2 g

Smashed Potatoes

Peppery Crispy Oven Fries

Chile-Lime Roasted Vegetables

13 g
CARB

SERVES	8
HANDS ON	20 min.
TOTAL	50 min.

Nonstick cooking spray
8 oz. small red potatoes, peeled (if desired) and cut into 1-inch pieces
2 medium carrots, peeled and cut into 1-inch pieces
1 large parsnip or turnip, peeled and cut into 1-inch pieces
1 medium onion, cut up
2 Tbsp. olive oil
½ tsp. kosher salt
½ tsp. ground chipotle chile pepper
2 large red and/or sweet peppers, cut into 1-inch pieces
1½ cups halved or quartered fresh button or cremini mushrooms
5 cloves garlic, peeled
1 lime, halved
Fresh cilantro leaves

1. Preheat oven to 450°F. Line a 15×10-inch baking pan with foil; coat foil with cooking spray. Place the next four ingredients (through onion) in prepared pan. Drizzle with 1 Tbsp. of the oil; sprinkle with ¼ tsp. each of the salt and ground chipotle pepper.
2. Roast 20 minutes. Stir vegetables; add the next three ingredients (through garlic). Drizzle with remaining 1 Tbsp. oil and sprinkle with remaining ¼ tsp. each salt and ground chipotle pepper. Roast 10 to 15 minutes more or until vegetables are tender and edges are browned.
3. Squeeze juice from lime over vegetables and top with cilantro.

PER SERVING (½ cup each) **CAL** 88, **FAT** 4 g (1 g sat. fat), **CHOL** 0 mg, **SODIUM** 142 mg, **CARB** 13 g (3 g fiber, 4 g sugars), **PRO** 2 g

Peppery Crispy Oven Fries

18 g
CARB

SERVES	4
HANDS ON	25 min.
TOTAL	55 min.

½ tsp. garlic powder
½ tsp. smoked paprika
¼ to ½ tsp. black pepper
¼ tsp. salt
1 lb. russet potatoes
2 Tbsp. olive oil
Nonstick cooking spray
Malt vinegar (optional)

1. Arrange two oven racks on the top and bottom third of the oven. Preheat oven to 350°F. In a bowl combine the first four ingredients (through salt).
2. Cut potatoes into ¼-inch-wide strips. Place potato strips in a large bowl; add enough cold water to cover potatoes. Stir well. Drain in a colander set in the sink. Repeat rinsing and draining two or three times until water runs clear. Drain again, gently tossing potatoes in colander to drain as much water as possible. Transfer potato strips to several layers of paper towels. Use additional paper towels to pat dry.
3. Dry the large bowl and return potatoes to bowl. Drizzle with oil; sprinkle with pepper mixture. Toss to coat.
4. Generously coat two large baking sheets with cooking spray. Arrange potatoes in a single layer on prepared baking sheets. Place one baking sheet on each oven rack. Bake 15 minutes. Remove baking sheets from oven. Increase oven temperature to 450ºF. Return baking sheets to oven. Bake 15 to 18 minutes more or until browned and crisp, turning potatoes once. If desired, serve with a sprinkle of malt vinegar.

PER SERVING (¾ cup each) **CAL** 146, **FAT** 7 g (1 g sat. fat), **CHOL** 0 mg, **SODIUM** 164 mg, **CARB** 18 g (3 g fiber, 1 g sugars), **PRO** 2 g

QUICK TIP When roasting an assortment of fresh vegetables, be sure to cut them into similar-size pieces so they cook and brown evenly.

Chile-Lime Roasted Vegetables

Roasted Indian Cauliflower

8g **CARB** | **SERVES** 8
| **HANDS ON** 15 min.
| **TOTAL** 45 min.

- 2 Tbsp. peanut oil
- 2 tsp. sugar
- 2 tsp. yellow or black mustard seeds
- 2 tsp. grated fresh ginger
- 1½ tsp. ground turmeric
- 1½ tsp. ground cumin
- 1 tsp. ground coriander
- ½ tsp. salt
- ¼ tsp. crushed red pepper
- 1 medium medium head cauliflower (about 1½ lb.), cut into florets (about 4½ cups)
- 2 small bunches baby carrots with tops (about 10 oz.), tops trimmed
- 2 Tbsp. snipped fresh cilantro Lime wedges

1. Preheat oven to 425°F. Line a 15×10-inch baking pan with foil. In a bowl combine the first nine ingredients (through crushed red pepper). Add cauliflower and carrots; toss to coat. Spread in prepared baking pan.

2. Roast about 30 minutes or until vegetables are tender and beginning to brown on edges, stirring twice. Sprinkle with cilantro and serve with lime wedges.

PER SERVING (¾ cup each) **CAL** 71, **FAT** 4 g (1 g sat. fat), **CHOL** 0 mg, **SODIUM** 188 mg, **CARB** 8 g (2 g fiber, 4 g sugars), **PRO** 2 g

Roasted Indian Cauliflower

Green Beans
Foil Pack

Green Beans Foil Pack

9 g
CARB

SERVES 4

HANDS ON 20 min.

TOTAL 45 min.

- 1 lb. fresh green beans and/or wax beans
- 3 small shallots, thinly sliced
- 3 cloves garlic, thinly sliced
- ¼ tsp. salt
- ¼ tsp. black pepper
- 1 Tbsp. olive oil

1. Remove stems and strings from beans. Fold a 36×18-inch piece of heavy foil in half to make an 18-inch square. Place beans, shallot, and garlic in center of foil. Sprinkle lightly with salt and pepper. Drizzle with olive oil. Bring up two opposite edges of foil; seal with a double fold. Fold remaining edges to completely enclose vegetables, leaving space for steam to build.

2. Grill packet, uncovered, over medium heat 25 to 30 minutes or until vegetables are tender, turning packet occasionally. Carefully open packet to allow steam to escape. Season to taste with additional salt and pepper.

PER SERVING *(¾ cup each)* **CAL** 67, **FAT** 4 g (0 g sat. fat), **CHOL** 0 mg, **SODIUM** 152 mg, **CARB** 9 g (3 g fiber, 2 g sugars), **PRO** 2 g

Squash, Corn, and Barley Succotash

23 g
CARB

SERVES	12
HANDS ON	15 min.
TOTAL	1 hr.

4	cups water
½	cup regular pearled barley
¾	tsp. salt
1	Tbsp. olive oil
1	cup finely chopped onion
1	lb. butternut squash, peeled, seeded, and cut into ½-inch cubes (about 4 cups)
¾	cup reduced-sodium chicken broth
¼	tsp. black pepper
⅛	tsp. dried thyme, crushed
3	cups frozen whole kernel corn
¼	cup chopped fresh parsley

1. In a medium saucepan bring the water to boiling. Add barley and ½ tsp. of the salt. Return to boiling; reduce heat. Cover and simmer about 40 minutes or until barley is tender, stirring occasionally. Drain.

2. Meanwhile, in 10-inch skillet heat oil over medium-high. Add onion; cook and stir about 5 minutes or until tender. Stir in squash, broth, pepper, thyme, and the remaining ¼ tsp. salt. Bring to boiling; reduce heat. Simmer, covered, about 10 minutes or until squash is tender. Stir in corn; cover and cook 5 minutes more. Stir in barley and parsley; heat through.

PER SERVING (½ cup each) **CAL** 109, **FAT** 2 g (0 g sat. fat), **CHOL** 0 mg, **SODIUM** 187 mg, **CARB** 23 g (4 g fiber, 3 g sugars), **PRO** 3 g

 QUICK TIP Butternut squash gives this dish a colorful and nutritious boost. Sweet potatoes make an equally delicious and healthful alternative to the squash.

Lemon-Tarragon Peas

Lemon-Tarragon Peas

14 g CARB

SERVES 6
HANDS ON 15 min.
TOTAL 30 min.

- ½ cup water
- 3½ cups shelled fresh English peas
- 1½ cups whole fresh sugar snap pea pods and/or snow pea pods
- 1 Tbsp. butter, softened
- 1 Tbsp. snipped fresh tarragon
- 2 tsp. lemon zest
- ½ tsp. freshly cracked black pepper
- ¼ tsp. salt

1. In a medium saucepan bring the water to boiling. Add English peas. Return to boiling; reduce heat. Simmer, covered, 8 minutes. Add the sugar snap peas. Cook, covered, about 4 minutes or just until crisp-tender; drain.

2. Add the remaining ingredients to the peas. Toss gently until butter melts. Serve immediately.

PER SERVING (½ cup each) **CAL** 91, **FAT** 2 g (1 g sat. fat), **CHOL** 4 mg, **SODIUM** 19 mg, **CARB** 14 g (5 g fiber, 0 g sugars), **PRO** 5 g

QUICK TIP

To shell English peas, cut both ends of the pea pods to remove the strings. Pop open the pods. Run your thumb down the length of the pods and pop out the peas.

Apple-Thyme Sauté

Apple-Thyme Sauté

15 g CARB

SERVES 4
TOTAL 15 min.

- 1 Tbsp. butter
- 2 medium Granny Smith and/or Rome Beauty apples, cored and cut into ½-inch wedges (about 2½ cups)
- ⅓ cup sliced shallots
- 1 Tbsp. snipped fresh thyme or 1 tsp. dried thyme, crushed
- 1 Tbsp. lemon juice
- ¼ tsp. salt
- ⅛ tsp. black pepper

1. In a 10-inch skillet melt butter over medium. Add apples, shallots, and thyme. Cook, covered, about 5 minutes or just until apples are tender, stirring occasionally. Stir in lemon juice, salt, and pepper.

PER SERVING (¾ cup each) **CAL** 84, **FAT** 3 g (2 g sat. fat), **CHOL** 8 mg, **SODIUM** 168 mg, **CARB** 15 g (2 g fiber, 10 g sugars), **PRO** 1 g

6

EYE-OPENING
BREAKFASTS

Get fueled for your day with warm and filling hot cereals; quick

to-go sandwiches, smoothies, and muffins; or more-relaxed

weekend-style fare like breakfast nachos, crepes, and an egg

casserole. These creative morning foods give you the boost you

need to power through to lunch.

Slow Cooker Overnight Oatmeal with Apples and Walnuts

Slow Cooker Overnight Oatmeal with Apples and Walnuts

34 g
CARB

SERVES 8
HANDS ON 20 min.
SLOW COOK 6 hr. (low)

- 4 cups chopped apples
- 2 cups fat-free milk
- 2 cups water
- 1 cup steel-cut oats
- ¼ cup packed brown sugar*
- 2 Tbsp. butter, sliced
- 1 tsp. vanilla
- ½ tsp. ground cinnamon
- ¼ tsp. salt
- ¼ tsp. ground nutmeg
- 2 tsp. canola oil
- 1 tsp. packed brown sugar*
- 1 tsp. lemon juice
- ½ cup chopped walnuts, toasted

1. Line a 3½- or 4-qt. slow cooker with a disposable slow cooker liner. In prepared cooker combine 2 cups of the apples and the next nine ingredients (through nutmeg). Cover and cook on low 6 to 8 hours.
2. Shortly before oatmeal is done, preheat oven to 450°F. For topping, in a 15×10-inch baking pan drizzle remaining 2 cups apples with oil; toss to coat. Roast 10 to 12 minutes or until lightly browned, stirring once. Stir in the 1 tsp. brown sugar and lemon juice.
3. Top servings of oatmeal with apple topping and walnuts.

*****Sugar Sub** We do not recommend a sugar sub for this recipe.

PER SERVING (⅔ cup oatmeal + 2 Tbsp. apple topping + 1 Tbsp. nuts each) **CAL** 248, **FAT** 10 g (3 g sat. fat), **CHOL** 9 mg, **SODIUM** 126 mg, **CARB** 34 g (4 g fiber, 16 g sugars), **PRO** 7 g

Farro, Almond, and Blueberry Hot Breakfast Cereal

Farro, Almond, and Blueberry Hot Breakfast Cereal

33 g
CARB

SERVES 3
HANDS ON 10 min.
TOTAL 12 hr.

- ½ cup whole grain farro
- 1 cup unsweetened almond milk
- ¼ tsp. kosher salt
- ¼ tsp. vanilla
  Dash ground cinnamon
- ½ cup fresh blueberries
- ¼ cup unsalted whole almonds, toasted and chopped
- 1 Tbsp. pure maple syrup
- ¼ tsp. lemon zest

1. In a bowl combine farro and enough water to cover. Soak in the refrigerator overnight. Drain off excess water.
2. In a small saucepan combine milk, salt, vanilla, and cinnamon. Bring to boiling. Stir in farro; reduce heat. Simmer, covered, about 20 minutes or until farro is tender.
3. Stir in blueberries, 2 Tbsp. of the almonds, the maple syrup, and lemon zest. Cover and let stand 5 minutes or until blueberries are warm. Spoon cereal into serving dishes. Sprinkle with the remaining 2 Tbsp. almonds.

Tip To toast nuts, spread in a shallow baking pan. Bake in a 350°F oven 5 to 10 minutes or until golden, shaking pan once or twice.

PER SERVING (⅔ cup each) **CAL** 226, **FAT** 7 g (0 g sat. fat), **CHOL** 0 mg, **SODIUM** 235 mg, **CARB** 33 g (4 g fiber, 7 g sugars), **PRO** 8 g

« QUICK TIP
Whole grain farro soaks in water overnight to soften and reduce cooking time in the morning.

Tropical Oatmeal

28 g
CARB

SERVES 2
TOTAL 10 min.

½ cup refrigerated unsweetened coconut milk beverage
¼ cup water
½ cup dry multigrain hot cereal
⅛ tsp. salt
½ tsp. vanilla

¼ cup plain fat-free Greek yogurt
¼ cup chopped mango
2 Tbsp. chopped macadamia nuts
2 tsp. shredded unsweetened coconut or raw chip coconut, toasted
2 tsp. honey

1. In a small saucepan bring coconut milk beverage and the water to boiling; stir in cereal and salt. Cook over medium-low 1 to 2 minutes or until liquid is absorbed, stirring occasionally. Stir in vanilla.

2. Top servings with the remaining ingredients.

PER SERVING *(1 cup oatmeal + toppers each)* **CAL** 223, **FAT** 11 g (5 g sat. fat), **CHOL** 0 mg, **SODIUM** 199 mg, **CARB** 28 g (4 g fiber, 11 g sugars), **PRO** 7 g

Pumpkin-Apple Smoothies

25 g
CARB

SERVES 4
TOTAL 10 min.

1½ cups unsweetened vanilla almond milk
1⅓ cups chopped apples (2 medium)
½ of a 15-oz. can pumpkin
¾ cup plain fat-free Greek yogurt
½ cup ice
2 Tbsp. pure maple syrup
¼ tsp. pumpkin pie spice
⅛ tsp. salt
¼ cup high-protein honey-almond-flavor granola

1. In a blender combine the first eight ingredients (through salt). Cover and blend until smooth. Top each serving with 1 Tbsp. of the granola.

PER SERVING *(1 cup each)* **CAL** 151, **FAT** 3 g (0 g sat. fat), **CHOL** 0 mg, **SODIUM** 173 mg, **CARB** 25 g (4 g fiber, 17 g sugars), **PRO** 8 g

QUICK TIP This brunch dish is easy on the cook. Assemble it the night before, chill, and bake the cheesy casserole the next morning.

Ham and Broccoli
Breakfast Casserole

Ham and Broccoli Breakfast Casserole

20 g
CARB

SERVES	8
HANDS ON	20 min.
TOTAL	12 hr.

- 2 cups broccoli florets
  Nonstick cooking spray
- 4 cups refrigerated shredded hash brown potatoes
- 2 Tbsp. coarsely snipped fresh chives
- 6 oz. thinly sliced lower-sodium cooked honey ham, chopped
- 1 cup shredded reduced-fat cheddar cheese
- 8 eggs, lightly beaten
- ½ cup fat-free milk
- ½ tsp. salt
- ½ tsp. black pepper
- ¼ tsp. garlic powder

1. In a medium saucepan cook broccoli in boiling, lightly salted water 3 minutes; drain. Rinse with cold water; drain again.

2. Coat a 2-qt. rectangular baking dish with cooking spray. Add potatoes and chives to prepared dish; toss to combine. Top with broccoli, ham, and cheese.

3. In a bowl combine the remaining ingredients. Pour egg mixture over potato mixture. Cover with foil and chill overnight.

4. To serve, preheat oven to 350°F. Bake, uncovered, 50 to 55 minutes or until eggs are set (160°F). If necessary to prevent overbrowning, cover with foil the last 10 minutes of baking.

PER SERVING (⅛ casserole each) **CAL** 219, **FAT** 9 g (4 g sat. fat), **CHOL** 206 mg, **SODIUM** 550 mg, **CARB** 20 g (2 g fiber, 2 g sugars), **PRO** 15 g

Lemon-Strawberry Chia Seed Muffins

Lemon-Strawberry Chia Seed Muffins

24 g
CARB

SERVES	12
HANDS ON	20 min.
TOTAL	40 min.

- Nonstick cooking spray
- ¼ cup water
- 2 Tbsp. chia seeds, ground
- ¾ cup low-fat (1%) milk
- ¼ cup canola oil
- ¼ cup plain fat-free Greek yogurt
- 1 cup all-purpose flour
- 1 cup regular rolled oats
- ½ cup sugar*
- 1 Tbsp. baking powder
- 1 Tbsp. lemon zest
- ¼ tsp. salt
- ½ cup chopped strawberries

1. Preheat oven to 375°F. Coat twelve 2½-inch muffin cups with cooking spray. In a bowl combine the water and chia seeds. Whisk in milk, oil, and yogurt.

2. In a medium bowl stir together the next six ingredients (through salt). Make a well in the center of flour mixture. Add chia mixture all at once to flour mixture; stir just until moistened (batter should be lumpy). Fold in strawberries. Spoon batter into the prepared muffin cups, filling each cup about three-fourths full.

3. Bake 15 to 20 minutes or until tops are lightly browned and a toothpick inserted near centers of muffins comes out clean. Cool in muffin cups on a wire rack 5 minutes. Remove from muffin cups. Serve warm.

***Sugar Sub** Choose Splenda Sugar Blend. Follow package directions to use ½ cup equivalent.

PER SERVING (1 muffin each) **CAL** 157, **FAT** 6 g (1 g sat. fat), **CHOL** 1 mg, **SODIUM** 180 mg, **CARB** 24 g (2 g fiber, 10 g sugars), **PRO** 3 g

PER SERVING WITH SUB Same as above, except **CAL** 144, **CARB** 19 g (5 g sugars)

Peaches 'n' Cream Crepes

Two-Bran Refrigerator Muffins

27 g **SERVES** 12
CARB **HANDS ON** 15 min.
TOTAL 35 min.

⅔ cup whole bran cereal
⅓ cup oat bran
⅔ cup boiling water
½ cup buttermilk
2 egg whites, lightly beaten
¼ cup unsweetened applesauce
¼ cup canola oil
1½ cups all-purpose flour
½ cup packed brown sugar*
1½ tsp. baking powder
1 tsp. ground cinnamon
¼ tsp. baking soda
¼ tsp. salt
Nonstick cooking spray

1. In a medium bowl stir together whole bran cereal and oat bran. Stir in the boiling water. Stir in buttermilk, egg whites, applesauce, and oil.
2. In a large bowl stir together the next six ingredients (through salt). Add cereal mixture all at once to flour mixture, stirring just until moistened. Place plastic wrap over the surface of the batter. Cover tightly; refrigerate up to 3 days (or bake immediately).
3. To bake, preheat oven to 400°F. Coat as many 2½-inch muffin cups with cooking spray as needed to bake desired number of muffins. Spoon batter into the prepared muffin cups, filling each two-thirds full. Bake about 20 minutes or until a toothpick inserted near the centers comes out clean. Remove from muffin cups; serve warm.

*Sugar Sub We do not recommend a sugar sub for this recipe.

PER SERVING *(1 muffin each)* CAL 158, FAT 5 g (0 g sat. fat), CHOL 0 mg, SODIUM 168 mg, CARB 27 g (2 g fiber, 11 g sugars), PRO 3 g

Peaches 'n' Cream Crepes

35 g **SERVES** 2
CARB **TOTAL** 10 min.

4 oz. reduced-fat cream cheese (neufchatel)
1 to 2 Tbsp. fat-free milk
2 cups frozen unsweetened peach slices, chopped
¼ tsp. apple pie spice
4 9-inch ready-to-use crepes
½ tsp. powdered sugar*

1. In a medium bowl microwave cream cheese about 10 seconds or until softened. Stir in enough of the milk to reach spreading consistency.

2. In another bowl microwave peaches 2 to 4 minutes or until thawed, stirring once. Remove ¼ cup of the peaches. Stir the remaining peaches and apple pie spice into cream cheese mixture.
3. Spoon one-fourth of the cream cheese mixture onto half of each crepe; fold into quarters. Top with the reserved peaches and dust with powdered sugar.

*Sugar Sub We do not recommend a sugar sub for this recipe.

PER SERVING *(2 crepes each)* CAL 301, FAT 15 g (8 g sat. fat), CHOL 54 mg, SODIUM 351 mg, CARB 35 g (2 g fiber, 23 g sugars), PRO 8 g

Two-Bran Refrigerator Muffins

Blueberry-Lemon Silver Dollar Pancakes

29 g **SERVES** 4
CARB **TOTAL** 10 min.

Nonstick cooking spray
½ cup low-fat cottage cheese
¼ cup fat-free milk
2 egg whites
½ tsp. lemon zest
1 cup heart-healthy pancake and baking mix
⅔ cup fresh blueberries
¼ cup sugar-free maple-flavor syrup
Fresh blueberries (optional)
Lemon zest (optional)

1. Lightly coat an unheated 12-inch nonstick griddle or electric pancake griddle with cooking spray. Heat the griddle over medium-high.
2. Meanwhile, in a medium bowl stir together cottage cheese, milk, egg whites, and the ½ tsp. lemon zest. Add pancake mix; stir until just combined. Gently stir in the ⅔ cup blueberries.
3. For each pancake, use a small ice cream scoop (2 Tbsp.) to spoon batter onto hot griddle; reduce heat to medium. If necessary, spread batter with back of the ice cream scoop. Cook 1 to 2 minutes per side or until pancakes are golden brown, turning with a spatula when surfaces are bubbly and edges are slightly dry.
4. Serve warm with syrup and, if desired, top with additional blueberries and lemon zest.

PER SERVING *(3 pancakes + 1 Tbsp. syrup each)* **CAL** 169, **FAT** 3 g (0 g sat. fat), **CHOL** 3 mg, **SODIUM** 478 mg, **CARB** 29 g (1 g fiber, 7 g sugars), **PRO** 8 g

Blueberry-Lemon Silver Dollar Pancakes

**Scrambled
Turkey Nachos**

Scrambled Turkey Nachos

22g
CARB

SERVES 2
TOTAL 10 min.

⅓ cup refrigerated fully cooked
   crumbled turkey sausage
   Nonstick cooking spray
⅓ cup refrigerated egg whites
2 oz. no-salt-added blue corn
   tortilla chips (about 24 chips)
¼ cup reduced-fat shredded
   sharp cheddar cheese
8 cherry tomatoes, quartered
   Snipped fresh cilantro
   (optional)

1. Heat turkey sausage in the
microwave according to package
directions; keep warm.
2. Coat an 8-inch nonstick skillet with
cooking spray. Heat the skillet over
medium-high. Add egg whites and
cook about 1 minute or until egg
whites are set, stirring occasionally.
3. Arrange chips on two plates. Top
with warm eggs, warm turkey, and
cheese. Microwave 20 to 30 seconds
or until cheese just melts. Top with
tomatoes. If desired, sprinkle with
cilantro.

PER SERVING (12 chips + ¼ cup cooked
eggs + 3 Tbsp. sausage + 2 Tbsp. cheese +
4 cherry tomatoes each) **CAL** 243,
FAT 12 g (3 g sat. fat), **CHOL** 23 mg,
SODIUM 314 mg, **CARB** 22 g (3 g fiber,
3 g sugars), **PRO** 13 g

QUICK TIP
Compare the
nutrition data on the
tortilla chip packages
to get the healthiest
one. It might even be
a yellow corn chip.

Curried Chicken Hash

27 g CARB | **SERVES** 2
TOTAL 10 min.

Nonstick cooking spray
2 tsp. olive oil
1½ cups refrigerated shredded hash brown potatoes

2 links refrigerated breakfast fully cooked chicken sausage, sliced
1 tsp. curry powder
⅛ tsp. salt
⅛ tsp. black pepper
2 Tbsp. snipped fresh Italian parsley
2 Tbsp. plain fat-free Greek yogurt

1. Lightly coat an unheated 10-inch nonstick skillet with cooking spray; add the oil. Heat over medium-high.
2. Spread potatoes and sausage in the skillet in an even layer. Gently press with the back of a wide spatula or pancake turner to form a cake. Sprinkle with curry powder, salt, and pepper. Cook 4 minutes, without stirring.

Curried Chicken Hash

3. Using the spatula, turn over mixture in large sections. Cook 4 minutes more. To serve, fold together the mixture. Sprinkle with parsley. Serve with yogurt. If desired, sprinkle with additional pepper.

PER SERVING *(¾ cup each)* **CAL** 212, **FAT** 8 g (2 g sat. fat), **CHOL** 25 mg, **SODIUM** 406 mg, **CARB** 27 g (2 g fiber, 2 g sugars), **PRO** 9 g

Breakfast Sausage
Sandwiches

Breakfast Sausage Sandwiches

33 g
CARB

SERVES 2
TOTAL 10 min.

- 2 light multigrain English muffins
- 2 frozen cooked turkey sausage patties
- 2 ½-oz. slices reduced-fat sharp cheddar cheese
- 4 tsp. mango chutney or low-sugar orange marmalade

1. Split and toast the English muffins. Meanwhile, microwave frozen sausage patties according to package directions.
2. While toasted muffins are warm, place a cheese slice on each English muffin bottom; top cheese with a sausage patty. Top sausage with chutney and English muffin tops.

PER SERVING *(1 sandwich each)* **CAL** 229, **FAT** 8 g (3 g sat. fat), **CHOL** 38 mg, **SODIUM** 612 mg, **CARB** 33 g (8 g fiber, 7 g sugars), **PRO** 15 g

TASTY OATMEAL TOPPERS

A warm, hearty bowl of oatmeal will keep you full and energized until lunchtime. Satisfy your taste buds and boost nutrition with these flavorful and inexpensive toppers.

SHOP SMART. Buy regular or old-fashioned rolled oats for the best texture in these recipes (most brands have similar nutritional values, so just pick up what you like). Give the cooked oats a stir before adding toppers.

Peach-Maple Oatmeal

Top **½ cup cooked regular rolled oats** with **¼ cup diced fresh peach** and **1 Tbsp. sugar-free maple-flavor syrup.**

SERVES 1. **CAL** 107, **CARB** 21 g (3 g fiber, 4 g sugars)

Cherry-Chocolate Oatmeal

Top **½ cup cooked regular rolled oats** with **¼ cup fresh sweet cherries, pitted,** and **2 tsp. mini semisweet chocolate pieces.**

SERVES 1. **CAL** 161, **CARB** 27 g (3 g fiber, 11 g sugars)

Blueberry-Almond Oatmeal

Top **½ cup cooked regular rolled oats** with **2 Tbsp. plain fat-free Greek yogurt, 2 Tbsp. fresh blueberries,** and **1 Tbsp. slivered almonds, toasted.**

SERVES 1. **CAL** 149, **CARB** 19 g (3 g fiber, 4 g sugars)

Peanut Butter and Strawberry Oatmeal
Stir **4 tsp. PB2 Powdered Peanut Butter** into
½ cup cooked regular rolled oats. Top with
2 Tbsp. sliced fresh strawberries and **1 tsp. honey.**

SERVES 1. **CAL** 140, **CARB** 25 g (4 g fiber, 8 g sugars)

Pear-Spiced Oatmeal
Stir **⅛ tsp. ground ginger** into **½ cup cooked regular
rolled oats.** Top with **¼ cup diced fresh pear** and
⅛ tsp. ground cinnamon.

SERVES 1. **CAL** 108, **CARB** 21 g (3 g fiber, 4 g sugars)

Apricot-Walnut Oatmeal
Stir **a pinch apple pie spice** into **½ cup cooked regular
rolled oats.** Top with **2 Tbsp. chopped dried apricots** and
2 tsp. chopped walnuts, toasted.

SERVES 1. **CAL** 155, **CARB** 25 g (4 g fiber, 9 g sugars)

Mocha-Raspberry Oatmeal
Stir **½ tsp. instant coffee crystals** into **½ cup cooked
regular rolled oats.** Top with **¼ cup fresh raspberries** and
1 Tbsp. sugar-free chocolate-flavor syrup.

SERVES 1. **CAL** 110, **CARB** 21 g (4 g fiber, 2 g sugars)

7

GOOD-FOR-YOU
SNACKS

Elect to have one of these tasty and creative snacks to satisfy

between-meal hunger without a sugar spike. These recipes strive

to keep fat and calories in check while providing a good balance of

carbs and protein to hold you until your next main meal.

Roasted Eggplant, Garlic, and Red Pepper Dip

12 g
CARB

SERVES 6	
HANDS ON 20 min.	
TOTAL 1 hr. 10 min.	

- 1 garlic bulb
- 1 medium eggplant, trimmed and halved lengthwise
- 1 medium red sweet pepper, halved lengthwise
- 1 Tbsp. olive oil
- ½ tsp. kosher salt
- ¼ tsp. smoked paprika
- ¼ tsp. black pepper
- 1 5.3-oz. carton plain fat-free Greek yogurt
- 2 tsp. olive oil
- 1 Tbsp. finely snipped fresh basil
- 12 celery stalks, cut into sticks

1. Preheat oven to 400°F. Cut off the top ½ inch of garlic bulb to expose ends of individual cloves. Leaving garlic bulb whole, remove any loose, papery outer layers. Brush garlic bulb, eggplant, and sweet pepper with the 1 Tbsp. oil.
2. Place garlic, cut end up, and eggplant and sweet pepper, skin sides up, on a baking sheet. Roast 50 minutes or until garlic feels soft when squeezed and eggplant and pepper are soft and starting to brown.
3. Using a spoon, scoop flesh from eggplant into a large bowl. If desired, remove the large seeds (in some eggplants they may taste bitter). Squeeze garlic paste from cloves into bowl with eggplant. Mash and/or chop mixture until desired consistency. Stir in ¼ tsp. of the salt, the smoked paprika, and black pepper.
4. Peel and discard skins from roasted pepper; chop pepper. In a bowl combine roasted pepper, yogurt, and the remaining ¼ tsp. salt.
5. In a small bowl microwave the 2 tsp. oil 20 to 30 seconds or until warm. Stir in basil.
6. Spoon eggplant mixture and yogurt mixture, side by side, into a serving bowl. Drizzle with basil oil. Serve dip with celery sticks.

PER SERVING (⅓ cup each) **CAL** 98, **FAT** 4 g (1 g sat. fat), **CHOL** 1 mg, **SODIUM** 241 mg, **CARB** 12 g (5 g fiber, 6 g sugars), **PRO** 5 g

Roasted Eggplant, Garlic, and Red Pepper Dip

Avocado Deviled Eggs

1g
CARB

SERVES 24
TOTAL 25 min.

- 12 eggs, hard-cooked and peeled
- ½ cup light mayonnaise
- 1 Tbsp. country Dijon-style mustard
- 2 tsp. lemon juice
- ⅛ tsp. freshly ground black pepper
  Dash hot pepper sauce
- 1 ripe, yet firm avocado, halved, seeded, and peeled
  Snipped fresh chives (optional)

1. Cut eggs in half lengthwise and remove yolks. Set whites aside. Place yolks in a large bowl; mash with a fork. Stir in mayonnaise, mustard, 1 tsp. of the lemon juice, the black pepper, and hot pepper sauce. Spoon or pipe yolk mixture into egg white halves. Cover and chill up to 4 hours.
2. Before serving, cut avocado into ½-inch pieces; toss gently with the remaining 1 tsp. lemon juice. Sprinkle deviled eggs with avocado and, if desired, chives.

Tip To hard-cook eggs, place eggs in a single layer in a 4-qt. Dutch oven. Add enough cold water to cover eggs by 1 inch. Bring to a full rolling boil over high heat; remove from heat. Cover and let stand 15 minutes; drain. Place eggs in ice water to cool; drain. To peel, gently tap each egg on countertop. Roll egg between the palms of your hands. Peel off eggshell, starting at the large end.

PER SERVING *(1 egg half each)* **CAL** 79, **FAT** 7 g (1 g sat. fat), **CHOL** 96 mg, **SODIUM** 71 mg, **CARB** 1 g (0 g fiber, 0 g sugars), **PRO** 3 g

Avocado Deviled Eggs

**Open-Face
Sandwich Bites**

Apple and Walnut Crostini with Balsamic Drizzle

Apple and Walnut Crostini with Balsamic Drizzle

14 g
CARB

SERVES 12
HANDS ON 25 min.
TOTAL 1 hr. 25 min.

- ½ cup Homemade Walnut Butter or walnut butter
- ½ cup balsamic vinegar
- 6 oz. whole grain baguette-style French bread
  Nonstick cooking spray
- 24 thin slices green apple
  Microgreens (optional)

1. If using, prepare Homemade Walnut Butter; chill as directed.
2. Preheat oven to 375°F. Line a baking sheet with parchment paper. In a small saucepan bring balsamic vinegar to boiling; reduce heat. Simmer, uncovered, about 12 minutes or until thickened and reduced to 2 to 3 Tbsp. (vinegar will thicken more as it cools).
3. Meanwhile, cut bread into 24 slices. Arrange bread slices in a single layer on the prepared baking sheet. Coat both sides of bread slices with cooking spray. Bake about 8 minutes or until toasted, turning once.
4. To assemble crostini, spread one side of each toasted bread slice with 1 tsp. of the walnut butter. Top each with 1 apple slice and drizzle each with about ¼ tsp. of the balsamic syrup. If desired, top with microgreens. Serve immediately.

Homemade Walnut Butter Place 3 cups walnut halves, toasted, in a food processor. Cover and process until finely chopped. Add 3 Tbsp. pure maple syrup, ⅛ tsp. salt, and a dash ground cinnamon. Cover and process 5 minutes more or until nearly smooth, stopping and scraping sides of bowl as needed. Cover and chill about 1 hour.

PER SERVING *(2 crostini each)* **CAL** 123, **FAT** 7 g (1 g sat. fat), **CHOL** 0 mg, **SODIUM** 97 mg, **CARB** 14 g (2 g fiber, 5 g sugars), **PRO** 3 g

Open-Face Sandwich Bites

12 g
CARB

SERVES 4
TOTAL 10 min.

- 8 slices dark pumpernickel party bread
- 2 light creamy Swiss individually foil-wrapped spreadable cheese wedges
- 2 slices lower-sodium, less-fat bacon, crisp-cooked according to package directions
- 8 blackberries, halved

1. Preheat broiler. Toast bread under broiler about 1 minute per side or until crisp.
2. Spread one-fourth of a cheese wedge on each bread slice. Top each with a ¼ slice bacon and 2 blackberry halves.

PER SERVING *(2 bites each)* **CAL** 87, **FAT** 2 g (1 g sat. fat), **CHOL** 4 mg, **SODIUM** 267 mg, **CARB** 12 g (2 g fiber, 1 g sugars), **PRO** 4 g

Pineapple Salsa
Bruschetta

Pineapple Salsa Bruschetta

16 g
CARB

SERVES 1
TOTAL 10 min.

- 4 tsp. reduced-fat garlic and herbs soft spreadable cheese
- 4 cinnamon-raisin bagel crisps
- 4 tsp. medium-hot pineapple salsa
  Snipped fresh chives

1. Spread 1 tsp. of the cheese on each bagel crisp. Top each with 1 tsp. pineapple salsa. Sprinkle with chives.

PER SERVING *(4 bruschetta each)* **CAL** 123, **FAT** 5 g (3 g sat. fat), **CHOL** 10 mg, **SODIUM** 220 mg, **CARB** 16 g (1 g fiber, 7 g sugars), **PRO** 3 g

Endive Leaf Bites

11 g
CARB

SERVES 2
TOTAL 10 min.

- 1 oz. goat cheese (chèvre), Brie, or cream cheese
- 4 Belgian endive leaves
- 4 dried apricots, sliced
- 4 tsp. roasted and salted pistachio nuts

1. Crumble or spread the cheese on top of the endive leaves. Sprinkle with the apricots and nuts.

PER SERVING *(2 leaf bites each)* **CAL** 119, **FAT** 7 g (3 g sat. fat), **CHOL** 11 mg, **SODIUM** 85 mg, **CARB** 11 g (2 g fiber, 8 g sugars), **PRO** 5 g

Endive Leaf Bites

Apple Multigrain Nachos

16 g
CARB

| **SERVES** 2 |
| **TOTAL** 10 min. |

14 multigrain tortilla chips
½ cup coarsely chopped apple
3 Tbsp. shredded reduced-fat
cheddar cheese
Dash apple pie spice

1. On a microwave-safe plate, arrange tortilla chips; top with apples and cheese.
2. Microwave about 1 minute or until cheese begins to melt. Sprinkle with apple pie spice. Serve warm.

PER SERVING (*7 chips + half of the toppings each*) **CAL** 124, **FAT** 5 g (2 g sat. fat), **CHOL** 8 mg, **SODIUM** 109 mg, **CARB** 16 g (3 g fiber, 6 g sugars), **PRO** 4 g

Cauliflower Hummus

5g CARB

SERVES 18
HANDS ON 25 min.
TOTAL 2 hr. 35 min.

1 medium head cauliflower (1½ to 2 lb.), cored and cut into florets (4 cups)
1 lemon
2 Tbsp. tahini (sesame seed paste)
2 Tbsp. olive oil
4 cloves garlic
½ tsp. ground cumin
½ tsp. salt
3 Tbsp. snipped fresh cilantro
¼ tsp. crushed red pepper
Broken flatbread, crackers, baked pita bread chips, cucumber slices, baby carrots, sweet pepper strips, and/or roma tomato wedges

1. In a covered large saucepan cook cauliflower in a small amount of boiling water about 10 minutes or until tender; drain. Transfer cauliflower to a bowl of ice water until cool; drain.

2. Remove 2 tsp. zest and squeeze 1 Tbsp. juice from lemon. In a food processor combine 1 tsp. of the lemon zest, the lemon juice, cooked cauliflower, and the next five ingredients (through salt). Cover and process until smooth. Add the cilantro and process 5 seconds. Transfer hummus to a serving bowl. Cover and chill 2 to 8 hours.

3. Just before serving, in a bowl stir together the remaining 1 tsp. lemon zest and the crushed red pepper. Sprinkle over hummus with additional snipped fresh cilantro. Serve with flatbread, crackers, and/or vegetables.

PER SERVING (2 Tbsp. each) **CAL** 52, **FAT** 3 g (0 g sat. fat), **CHOL** 0 mg, **SODIUM** 107 mg, **CARB** 5 g (1 g fiber, 1 g sugars), **PRO** 1 g

QUICK TIP Look for very small heads of Bibb or Boston lettuce to create these delicate snacks. If you like, use larger leaves and make only two lettuce cups.

Egg Salad Stuffed
Lettuce Cups

Curried Chive Dip with Veggies

Egg Salad Stuffed Lettuce Cups

4 g
CARB

SERVES 2
TOTAL 10 min.

- 2 hard-cooked eggs, chopped (tip, *p. 131*)
- ½ cup finely chopped celery with leaves
- 2 Tbsp. fat-free mayonnaise
- ¼ tsp. salt-free Cajun or Creole seasoning
- ⅛ tsp. bottled hot pepper sauce
- 4 small butterhead (Bibb or Boston) lettuce leaves or 8 Belgian endive leaves
  Red radish, thinly sliced (optional)
  Smoked paprika (optional)

1. In a small bowl combine the first five ingredients (through hot pepper sauce). Spoon mixture into lettuce leaves. If desired, top with radish, additional hot pepper sauce, and/or smoked paprika.

PER SERVING *(2 lettuce cups each)* **CAL** 97, **FAT** 6 g (2 g sat. fat), **CHOL** 188 mg, **SODIUM** 208 mg, **CARB** 4 g (2 g fiber, 2 g sugars), **PRO** 7 g

Curried Chive Dip with Veggies

5 g
CARB

SERVES 8
TOTAL 10 min.

- ½ of an 8-oz. carton whipped cream cheese spread with chives
- ¼ cup finely chopped yellow sweet pepper
- ¼ cup fat-free milk
- ½ tsp. curry powder
- ⅛ tsp. garlic powder
  Dash black pepper
- 4 cups vegetable dippers, such as cauliflower, carrots, broccoli, and/or sweet peppers

1. In a bowl combine the first six ingredients (through black pepper). Serve with assorted vegetable dippers.

PER SERVING *(2 Tbsp. dip + ½ cup vegetable dippers each)* **CAL** 50, **FAT** 3 g (2 g sat. fat), **CHOL** 10 mg, **SODIUM** 79 mg, **CARB** 5 g (1 g fiber, 2 g sugars), **PRO** 2 g

Popcorn
Crunch Mix

Popcorn Crunch Mix

18 g
CARB

SERVES 7
TOTAL 15 min.

2 cups honey-nut cereal
4 cups light sea-salt popcorn
½ cup cocoa peanuts (2½ oz.)
1 oz. bittersweet chocolate

1. Line a large shallow pan with waxed paper or parchment paper. Add honey-nut cereal, popcorn, and peanuts to pan; gently toss to combine.
2. In a custard cup microwave chocolate on 50% power (medium) about 1 minute or until melted and smooth, stirring once. Drizzle over the cereal mixture. Freeze 5 minutes. Store in an airtight container in the refrigerator up to 2 days.

PER SERVING *(1 cup each)* **CAL** 140, **FAT** 7 g (2 g sat. fat), **CHOL** 0 mg, **SODIUM** 109 mg, **CARB** 18 g (2 g fiber, 7 g sugars), **PRO** 4 g

Peanut-Apple Balls

8g
CARB

SERVES	15
HANDS ON	25 min.
TOTAL	1 hr. 25 min.

½ cup chunky peanut butter
2 Tbsp. honey
2 cups rice and wheat cereal flakes
⅓ cup snipped dried apples
⅛ tsp. apple pie spice

1. In a large bowl stir together peanut butter and honey. Stir in cereal, snipped dried apples, and apple pie spice. Chill mixture until easy to handle (about 1 hour). Shape mixture into 15 balls. Store in an airtight container in the refrigerator.

PER SERVING (1 ball each) **CAL** 79, **FAT** 4 g (1 g sat. fat), **CHOL** 0 mg, **SODIUM** 73 mg, **CARB** 8 g (1 g fiber, 5 g sugars), **PRO** 3 g

POPCORN PLAY

Whether you're craving a savory snack or a sweet dessert, these popcorn perk-ups are sure to satisfy. You'll keep your calories in check—they're all 131 calories or less—with crunchy satisfaction.

SHOP SMART. Ditch store-bought butter-flavor microwave popcorn for the plain air-popped version—a covered pot and a stove top or an air popper are all you need to make it. You'll save about 27 calories, 3 g fat, and 65 mg sodium per cup when you do.

Dark Chocolate and Peanut Popcorn
In a small bowl combine **1 cup air-popped popcorn** and **1 Tbsp. roasted, salted peanuts**. Drizzle with **¼ oz. dark chocolate, melted**. Toss to combine.

SERVES 1. CAL 120, CARB 12 g (3 g fiber, 3 g sugars)

Salted Caramel and Pretzel Popcorn
In a small bowl combine **1 cup air-popped popcorn** and **½ oz. mini pretzel twists**. Drizzle with **2 tsp. sugar-free caramel topping** and sprinkle with **a dash salt**. Toss to combine.

SERVES 1. CAL 116, CARB 27 g (1 g fiber, 0 g sugars)

Italian Popcorn
Place **1 cup air-popped popcorn** in a small bowl and lightly coat with **nonstick butter-flavor cooking spray**. Add **1 Tbsp. grated Parmesan cheese** and **¼ Tbsp. Italian seasoning, crushed**. Toss to combine.

SERVES 1. CAL 52, CARB 7 g (1 g fiber, 0 g sugars)

Sweet Chili Popcorn

In a small bowl combine **1 cup air-popped popcorn**, **2 tsp. honey**, and **1 tsp. chili powder**. Toss to combine.

SERVES 1. **CAL** 81, **CARB** 19 g (2 g fiber, 12 g sugars)

Tropical Popcorn

In a small bowl combine **1 cup air-popped popcorn**, **2 Tbsp. snipped dried pineapple**, and **1 Tbsp. unsweetened coconut flakes, toasted**. Toss to combine.

SERVES 1. **CAL** 126, **CARB** 24 g (2 g fiber, 14 g sugars)

Cranberry White Chocolate Popcorn

In a small bowl combine **1 cup air-popped popcorn** and **1 Tbsp. chopped dried cranberries**. Drizzle with **½ oz. white chocolate, melted**. Toss to combine.

SERVES 1. **CAL** 131, **CARB** 21 g (2 g fiber, 14 g sugars)

BBQ Popcorn

In a small bowl combine **1 cup air-popped popcorn** and **10 bite-size cheese crackers**. Lightly coat with **nonstick butter-flavor cooking spray**. Sprinkle with **¼ tsp. barbecue seasoning**. Toss to combine.

SERVES 1. **CAL** 87, **CARB** 13 g (1 g fiber, 0 g sugars)

DELIGHTFUL
DESSERTS

8

Dessert is on the table if it fits in your meal plan and you are

careful about portion size. These treats were created with carb

and sugar content in mind, yet they still taste deliciously sweet

and indulgent. Enjoy a simple weekday cookie or a celebration-

worthy layer cake.

Hazelnut-Fig Biscotti with Apple Drizzle

16 g CARB

SERVES 30
HANDS ON 30 min.
TOTAL 2 hr. 20 min.

- ⅔ cup boiling water
- ½ cup dried figs, stemmed
- ¼ cup butter, softened
- ½ cup granulated sugar*
- 1 tsp. baking powder
- ¼ tsp. ground cardamom
- ½ cup refrigerated or frozen egg product, thawed, or 2 eggs
- 1 tsp. vanilla
- 1½ cups all-purpose flour
- ½ cup whole wheat pastry flour
- ½ cup finely chopped, toasted hazelnuts
- 1 recipe Apple Drizzle

1. Preheat oven to 375°F. Lightly grease a large cookie sheet. In a bowl combine boiling water and figs; cover and let stand 10 minutes. Drain; finely chop figs.
2. In a large bowl beat butter with a mixer on medium 30 seconds. Add sugar, baking powder, and cardamom; beat until combined. Beat in eggs and vanilla. Beat in flour. Stir in hazelnuts and figs.
3. Divide dough in half. Shape each portion into an 8-inch-long log. Place logs 3 inches apart on prepared cookie sheet; do not flatten logs. Bake 25 to 30 minutes or until firm and a toothpick inserted near centers of logs comes out clean. Cool on cookie sheet on a wire rack 1 hour.
4. Preheat oven to 325°F. Using a serrated knife, cut each log crosswise into ½-inch-thick slices. Arrange slices, cut sides down, on large cookie sheets. Bake 12 minutes; turn slices. Bake 11 to 13 minutes more or until dry and crisp. Remove; cool on wire racks. Before serving, drizzle Apple Drizzle over biscotti.

Apple Drizzle In a bowl combine 1 cup powdered sugar* and ¼ tsp. apple pie spice. Stir in 1 to 2 Tbsp. apple brandy or apple juice until smooth.

*Sugar Sub Choose Splenda Sugar Blend. Follow package directions to use ½ cup granulated sugar equivalent. We do not recommend a sugar sub for the powdered sugar in the drizzle.

PER SERVING (1 biscotti each) **CAL** 94, **FAT** 3 g (1 g sat. fat), **CHOL** 4 mg, **SODIUM** 37 mg, **CARB** 16 g (1 g fiber, 9 g sugars), **PRO** 2 g

PER SERVING WITH SUB Same as above, except **CAL** 89, **CARB** 14 g (7 g sugars)

Strawberry-Covered Chocolate Angel Food Cake

29 g CARB

SERVES 16
HANDS ON 30 min.
TOTAL 1 hr. 5 min.

- 1 cup cake flour
- ¼ cup unsweetened cocoa powder
- 1½ cups egg whites, room temperature
- 1 tsp. cream of tartar
- 1 tsp. vanilla
- 1¼ cups sugar*
- 4 cups sliced strawberries
- 2 Tbsp. sugar*
- 1 oz. shaved semisweet chocolate

1. Sift flour and cocoa powder together three times. Adjust baking rack to the lowest position in oven. Preheat oven to 350°F. In an extra-large bowl beat egg whites, cream of tartar, and vanilla with a mixer on medium until soft peaks form (tips

Hazelnut-Fig Biscotti with Apple Drizzle

**Strawberry-Covered
Chocolate Angel Food Cake**

curl). Gradually add the 1¼ cups sugar, 2 Tbsp. at a time, beating until stiff peaks form (tips stand straight).

2. Sift about one-fourth of the flour mixture over beaten egg whites; fold in gently. Repeat, folding in remaining flour mixture by fourths. Pour into an ungreased 10-inch tube pan. Gently cut through batter with a thin metal spatula to remove any air pockets.

3. Bake 35 to 45 minutes or until top springs back when lightly touched. Immediately invert cake; cool thoroughly in the pan. Loosen sides of cake from pan; remove cake.

4. Meanwhile, in a bowl combine half of the strawberries and the 2 Tbsp. sugar; lightly mash. Fold in remaining strawberries. Cover and chill until needed.

5. Spoon strawberry mixture over cake. Top with shaved chocolate.

*Sugar Sub We do not recommend a sugar sub for this recipe.

PER SERVING *(1 slice each)* **CAL** 134, **FAT** 1 g (0 g sat. fat), **CHOL** 0 mg, **SODIUM** 39 mg, **CARB** 29 g (1 g fiber, 20 g sugars), **PRO** 4 g

Coconut Cream and Fruit-Topped Vanilla Cake

30 g
CARB

SERVES 16
HANDS ON 45 min.
TOTAL 1 hr. 20 min.

1 Tbsp. honey
⅛ tsp. ground ginger
   Pinch ground cardamom
1 recipe Vanilla Cake
1 recipe Coconut Cream Frosting

1 cup assorted fresh fruit (such as raspberries, halved strawberries, coarsely chopped mango, coarsely chopped pineapple, and/or sliced kiwifruit)
2 Tbsp. large flaked unsweetened coconut, toasted

1. In a bowl stir together honey, ginger, and cardamom.

2. To assemble, place one cake layer on a cake platter. Spread with half of the Coconut Cream Frosting. Repeat layers. Toss fruit with honey mixture and arrange on cake. Sprinkle with coconut. Serve immediately.

Vanilla Cake In a small saucepan combine ¾ cup fat-free milk and ¼ cup butter. Using a sharp knife, split ½ of a vanilla bean lengthwise in half. Scrape

**Coconut Cream and
Fruit-Topped Vanilla Cake**

Pineapple Oatmeal Upside-Down Cake

28 g CARB

SERVES 12
HANDS ON 20 min.
TOTAL 1 hr. 30 min.

- 2 Tbsp. light stick butter
- ¼ cup packed brown sugar*
- ¼ cup chopped dry-roasted macadamia nuts
- 4 ¼-inch-thick slices peeled and cored fresh pineapple (6 oz.)
- 1¼ cups all-purpose flour
- ½ cup packed brown sugar*
- ⅓ cup quick-cooking rolled oats
- 1 tsp. baking powder
- ¾ tsp. apple pie spice
- ½ tsp. baking soda
- ½ cup buttermilk
- ¼ cup canola oil
- ¼ cup refrigerated or frozen egg product, thawed, or 1 egg, lightly beaten
- 1 tsp. vanilla

1. Preheat oven to 350°F. Place butter in a 9-inch round cake pan. Place pan in oven about 5 minutes or until butter melts. Tilt pan to evenly coat with butter. Sprinkle the bottom of pan with the ¼ cup brown sugar. Sprinkle with nuts. Arrange pineapple on top of nuts in pan.
2. In a bowl combine the next six ingredients (through baking soda); make a well in center of flour mixture. Add the remaining ingredients. Stir just until combined (batter may be slightly lumpy). Spoon batter over pineapple slices, spreading evenly.
3. Bake about 35 minutes or until a toothpick inserted all the way through in the center comes out clean. Cool in pan 5 minutes. Loosen sides of cake; invert onto cake platter. Cool 30 minutes; serve warm.

***Sugar Sub** We do not recommend a sugar sub for this recipe.

PER SERVING (1 slice each) **CAL** 192, **FAT** 8 g (1 g sat. fat), **CHOL** 3 mg, **SODIUM** 134 mg, **CARB** 28 g (1 g fiber, 16 g sugars), **PRO** 3 g

---

seeds from the halves into milk mixture. Add bean halves to saucepan. Heat over medium until butter is melted and milk is steaming, stirring occasionally (do not boil). Remove from the heat. Preheat oven to 350°F. Meanwhile, grease and lightly flour two 8-inch round cake pans. In a large bowl beat 3 eggs, room temperature, with a mixer on high about 4 minutes or until thickened and light yellow in color. Gradually add 1¼ cups sugar,* beating on medium 4 to 5 minutes or until light and fluffy. Add 1½ cups all-purpose flour, 1½ tsp. baking powder, and ¼ tsp. salt. Beat on low to medium just until combined. Remove the vanilla bean halves from milk mixture; discard. Add milk mixture to batter along with 1½ tsp. vanilla, beating until combined. Divide batter between prepared pans, spreading evenly. Bake about 25 minutes or until a toothpick inserted

near centers comes out clean. Cool cake layers in pans 10 minutes. Remove layers from pans; cool on wire racks.

Coconut Cream Frosting In a bowl beat 4 oz. reduced-fat cream cheese (neufchatel), softened, on medium until smooth. Beat in 2 Tbsp. unsweetened refrigerated coconut milk until smooth. If desired, beat in ¼ tsp. coconut extract. Fold in 1 cup frozen light whipped dessert topping, thawed.

***Sugar Sub** Choose Splenda Sugar Blend. Follow package directions to use 1¼ cups equivalent.

PER SERVING (1 slice each) **CAL** 189, **FAT** 6 g (4 g sat. fat), **CHOL** 48 mg, **SODIUM** 148 mg, **CARB** 30 g (1 g fiber, 19 g sugars), **PRO** 4 g

PER SERVING WITH SUB Same as above, except **CAL** 166, **CARB** 22 g (11 g sugars)

Pineapple Oatmeal Upside-Down Cake

QUICK TIP If you have whole chia seeds, grind them using a spice grinder or a mortar and pestle.

**Chocolate Chip
Oatmeal Bars**

Chocolate Chip Oatmeal Bars

20 g CARB

SERVES 24
HANDS ON 20 min.
TOTAL 1 hr.

¼ cup water
1½ tsp. ground chia seeds
1 cup regular rolled oats
1 cup white whole wheat flour
½ tsp. salt
½ tsp. baking powder
½ tsp. baking soda
¼ cup butter, softened
¾ cup packed brown sugar*
⅓ cup granulated sugar*
¼ cup refrigerated or frozen egg product, thawed, or 1 egg, lightly beaten
1 tsp. vanilla
1 cup semisweet chocolate pieces

1. Preheat oven to 350°F. Line a 13×9-inch baking pan with foil-lined parchment pan lining paper.
2. In a bowl combine the water and chia seeds; let stand 20 minutes.
3. Meanwhile, place ½ cup of the oats in a food processor. Cover and process until finely ground. Add the next four ingredients (through baking soda). Cover and process until combined.
4. In a large bowl beat butter and sugars with a mixer on medium until mixture starts to cling to the sides of the bowl. Beat in egg product, vanilla, and chia mixture until combined. Add the remaining ½ cup oats and the flour mixture, beating on low to medium until combined. Stir in chocolate pieces (dough will be stiff). Spread dough in the prepared pan.
5. Bake 18 to 20 minutes or until edges are golden. Cool in pan on a wire rack. Cut into 24 bars.

*Sugar Sub Choose Splenda Brown Sugar Blend for the brown sugar and Splenda Sugar Blend for the granulated sugar. Follow package directions to use ¾ cup brown sugar and ⅓ cup granulated sugar equivalents.

Blueberry Muffin Bars

PER SERVING (1 bar each) **CAL** 121, **FAT** 4 g (3 g sat. fat), **CHOL** 5 mg, **SODIUM** 108 mg, **CARB** 20 g (1 g fiber, 14 g sugars), **PRO** 2 g

PER SERVING WITH SUB Same as above, except **CAL** 91, **SODIUM** 106 mg, **CARB** 12 g (6 g sugars)

Blueberry Muffin Bars

15 g CARB

SERVES 32
HANDS ON 25 min.
TOTAL 55 min.

Nonstick cooking spray
1¾ cups quick-cooking rolled oats
¾ cup all-purpose flour
¾ cup whole wheat flour
¾ cup packed brown sugar*
1 tsp. apple pie spice
½ cup light butter
½ cup coarsely chopped slivered almonds
1 cup sugar-free blueberry preserves
½ tsp. almond extract

1. Preheat oven to 350°F. Line a 13×9-inch baking pan with foil, extending foil over the edges of the pan. Lightly coat foil with cooking spray.
2. In a large bowl combine the next five ingredients (through apple pie spice). Using a pastry blender, cut in butter until mixture is crumbly. Transfer ¾ cup of the crumb mixture to a small bowl; stir in almonds. Press the remaining crumb mixture into bottom of the prepared pan. Bake 10 minutes.
3. Meanwhile, in a bowl stir together the preserves and almond extract. Carefully spread preserves evenly over hot crust. Sprinkle with reserved crumb mixture; press lightly.
4. Bake 20 to 25 minutes or until top is lightly browned. Cool in pan on wire rack. Using the edges of the foil, lift uncut bars out of the pan. Cut into 32 bars.

*Sugar Sub We do not recommend a sugar sub for this recipe.

PER SERVING (1 bar each) **CAL** 89, **FAT** 3 g (1 g sat. fat), **CHOL** 4 mg, **SODIUM** 18 mg, **CARB** 15 g (1 g fiber, 5 g sugars), **PRO** 2 g

Berry-Rhubarb
Chocolate Crumble

Berry-Rhubarb Chocolate Crumble

31 g
CARB

SERVES 12	
HANDS ON 30 min.	
TOTAL 1 hr. 40 min.	

4   oz. chocolate biscotti, crushed
⅓   cup all-purpose flour
¼   cup packed brown sugar*
3   Tbsp. whole wheat flour
¼   tsp. salt
¼   cup butter, cut into cubes
⅓   cup granulated sugar*
¼   cup packed brown sugar*
2   Tbsp. all-purpose flour
1   tsp. vanilla
3   cups halved fresh strawberries
2   cups sliced fresh rhubarb
1   cup fresh raspberries

Nonstick cooking spray
¾   cup frozen light whipped dessert topping, thawed (optional)

1. Preheat oven to 350°F. For topping, in a bowl combine the first five ingredients (through salt). Using your fingers, work butter into biscotti mixture until incorporated.
2. In another bowl stir together the next four ingredients (through vanilla). Add fruit; toss gently to coat.
3. Coat a 2-qt. shallow baking dish with cooking spray. Transfer fruit mixture to prepared dish. Sprinkle with topping.
4. Bake about 40 minutes or until filling is thickened and bubbly. Cool 30 minutes before serving. If desired, serve with whipped topping and sprinkle with additional crushed biscotti.

*Sugar Sub Choose Splenda Brown Sugar Blend for the brown sugar and Splenda Sugar Blend for the granulated sugar. Follow package directions to use ½ cup brown sugar equivalent, dividing it between the topping and filling, and ⅓ cup granulated sugar equivalent.

PER SERVING (⅓ cup each) **CAL** 180, **FAT** 6 g (3 g sat. fat), **CHOL** 20 mg, **SODIUM** 114 mg, **CARB** 31 g (2 g fiber, 20 g sugars), **PRO** 2 g

PER SERVING WITH SUB Same as above, except **CAL** 156, **CARB** 23 g (12 g sugars)

PB&J Turnovers

20 g
CARB

SERVES	8
HANDS ON	30 min.
TOTAL	45 min.

- 1 cup all-purpose flour
- ⅓ cup whole wheat flour
- ¼ tsp. salt
- ¼ cup cold butter, cut up
- 6 to 7 Tbsp. cold water
- 4 tsp. natural creamy peanut butter
- ⅓ cup low-sugar grape jelly
- 1 egg, lightly beaten
- 1 Tbsp. water
- 1 tsp. coarse sugar (optional)*

1. Preheat oven to 425°F. Line a large baking sheet with foil.

2. In a bowl stir together flours and salt. Using a pastry blender, cut in butter until pieces are pea size. Sprinkle 1 Tbsp. cold water over part of the flour mixture; gently toss with a fork. Push moistened dough to the side of the bowl. Repeat moistening flour mixture, using 1 Tbsp. cold water at a time, until all flour mixture is moistened. Shape dough into a ball.

3. On a lightly floured surface, roll dough into a 16×8-inch rectangle, using your hands to shape the dough into a perfect rectangle. Using a fluted pastry wheel or pizza cutter, cut rectangle into eight 4-inch squares.

4. Spread ½ tsp. peanut butter on each square. Top each with 2 tsp. jelly. Fold squares in half to create triangles. Using a fork, press edges to seal. Place filled triangles 2 inches apart on the prepared baking sheet. Make one or two small slits in the top of each triangle. In a bowl combine egg and the 1 Tbsp. water. Brush egg mixture over tops of triangles. If desired, sprinkle with sugar.

5. Bake 12 to 14 minutes or until lightly browned. Transfer pies to a wire rack.

***Sugar Sub** We do not recommend a sugar sub for this recipe.

PER SERVING (1 turnover each) **CAL** 167, **FAT** 8 g (4 g sat. fat), **CHOL** 39 mg, **SODIUM** 137 mg, **CARB** 20 g (1 g fiber, 4 g sugars), **PRO** 4 g

PB&J Turnovers

Mexican Chocolate Pudding

25g CARB	**SERVES** 2
	HANDS ON 20 min.
	TOTAL 2 hr. 20 min.

- 2 Tbsp. sugar*
- 1½ Tbsp. unsweetened cocoa powder
- 1½ tsp. cornstarch
  Dash salt
- 1 cup fat-free milk
- 1 egg yolk, lightly beaten
- ½ tsp. vanilla
- ¼ tsp. ground cinnamon
  Dash cayenne pepper
- 2 Tbsp. frozen light whipped dessert topping, thawed

1. In a small heavy saucepan stir together sugar, cocoa powder, cornstarch, and salt. Whisk in milk. Cook and stir over medium until slightly thickened and bubbly. Cook and stir 2 minutes more. Remove from heat.

2. Gradually whisk about half of the hot mixture into egg yolk. Return egg yolk mixture to the remaining hot mixture in saucepan. Bring to a gentle boil; reduce heat. Cook and stir 1 minute more. Remove from heat. Stir in vanilla, cinnamon, and cayenne pepper.

3. Pour pudding into two dessert bowls. Cover surface of pudding with plastic wrap. Chill 2 to 24 hours before serving. Top each serving with 1 Tbsp. of the whipped topping and, if desired, sprinkle with additional ground cinnamon.

*Sugar Sub We do not recommend a sugar sub for this recipe.

PER SERVING (½ cup pudding + 1 Tbsp. dessert topping each) **CAL** 148, **FAT** 3 g (2 g sat. fat), **CHOL** 95 mg, **SODIUM** 94 mg, **CARB** 25 g (2 g fiber, 20 g sugars), **PRO** 6 g

Mexican Chocolate Pudding

Vanilla Ice Cream Sandwiches

26 g
CARB

SERVES 24
HANDS ON 45 min.
TOTAL 1 hr.

4 oz. reduced-fat cream cheese (neufchatel), softened
½ cup butter, softened
1¾ cups sugar*
1 tsp. baking soda
1 tsp. cream of tartar
⅛ tsp. salt
3 egg yolks
½ tsp. vanilla bean paste or vanilla
1¼ cups all-purpose flour
½ cup white whole wheat flour
3 cups reduced-fat vanilla ice cream, softened

1. Preheat oven to 300°F. In a large bowl beat cream cheese and butter with a mixer on medium 30 seconds. Add the next four ingredients (through salt). Beat until combined, scraping bowl as needed. Beat in egg yolks and vanilla bean paste. Beat in both flours.
2. Shape dough into 1-inch balls. Place balls 2 inches apart on an ungreased cookie sheet lined with parchment paper.
3. Bake 14 to 16 minutes or until edges are set but not brown. Cool on cookie sheet 1 minute. Remove; cool on a wire rack.
4. Spread ice cream on bottoms of half of the cookies, using 2 Tbsp. for each cookie. Top with remaining cookies, bottom sides down.

*Sugar Sub Choose Splenda Sugar Blend. Follow package directions to use 1¾ cups equivalent.

To Store Place sandwich cookies in a shallow baking pan and freeze at least 2 hours or until firm. Transfer to a freezer container and freeze up to 1 month.

PER SERVING (1 sandwich cookie each) **CAL** 167, **FAT** 6 g (4 g sat. fat), **CHOL** 39 mg, **SODIUM** 136 mg, **CARB** 26 g (0 g fiber, 18 g sugars), **PRO** 2 g

PER SERVING WITH SUB Same as above, except **CAL** 145, **CARB** 18 g (11 g sugars)

RECIPE INDEX

N–O

RECIPE GUIDE

Test Kitchen

High-standards testing
This seal assures you every recipe in this book has been tested by the *Better Homes and Gardens® Diabetic Living®* Test Kitchen. This means each recipe is practical, reliable, and meets our high standards of taste appeal.

Inside our recipes
We list precise serving sizes to help you manage portions. Test Kitchen tips and sugar subs are listed after recipe directions. If kitchen basics such as ice, salt, black pepper, oil, and nonstick cooking spray are not listed in the ingredients list, then they are italicized in the directions.

Nutrition information
Nutrition facts per serving are noted with each recipe; ingredients listed as optional are not included. When ingredient choices appear, we use the first one to calculate nutrition analysis.

Key to abbreviations
CAL = calories
CARB = carbohydrate
CHOL = cholesterol
PRO = protein

METRIC INFORMATION

The charts on this page provide a guide for converting measurements from the U.S. customary system, which is used throughout this book, to the metric system.

Product Differences

Most of the ingredients called for in the recipes in this book are available in most countries. However, some are known by different names. Here are some common American ingredients and their possible counterparts:

* All-purpose flour is enriched, bleached or unbleached white household flour. When self-rising flour is used in place of all-purpose flour in a recipe that calls for leavening, omit the leavening agent (baking soda or baking powder) and salt.
* Baking soda is bicarbonate of soda.
* Cornstarch is cornflour.
* Golden raisins are sultanas.
* Light-color corn syrup is golden syrup.
* Powdered sugar is icing sugar.
* Sugar (white) is granulated, fine granulated, or castor sugar.
* Vanilla or vanilla extract is vanilla essence.

Volume and Weight

The United States traditionally uses cup measures for liquid and solid ingredients. The chart below shows the approximate imperial and metric equivalents. If you are accustomed to weighing solid ingredients, the following approximate equivalents will be helpful.

* 1 cup butter, castor sugar, or rice = 8 ounces = $1/2$ pound = 250 grams
* 1 cup flour = 4 ounces = $1/4$ pound = 125 grams
* 1 cup icing sugar = 5 ounces = 150 grams

Canadian and U.S. volume for a cup measure is 8 fluid ounces (237 ml), but the standard metric equivalent is 250 ml.

1 British imperial cup is 10 fluid ounces.

In Australia, 1 tablespoon equals 20 ml, and there are 4 teaspoons in the Australian tablespoon.

Spoon measures are used for smaller amounts of ingredients. Although the size of the tablespoon varies slightly in different countries, for practical purposes and for recipes in this book, a straight substitution is all that's necessary. Measurements made using cups or spoons always should be level unless stated otherwise.

Common Weight Range Replacements

Imperial / U.S.	Metric
$1/2$ ounce	15 g
1 ounce	25 g or 30 g
4 ounces ($1/4$ pound)	115 g or 125 g
8 ounces ($1/2$ pound)	225 g or 250 g
16 ounces (1 pound)	450 g or 500 g
$1^1/4$ pounds	625 g
$1^1/2$ pounds	750 g
2 pounds or $2^1/4$ pounds	1,000 g or 1 Kg

Oven Temperature Equivalents

Fahrenheit Setting	Celsius Setting*	Gas Setting
300°F	150°C	Gas Mark 2 (very low)
325°F	160°C	Gas Mark 3 (low)
350°F	180°C	Gas Mark 4 (moderate)
375°F	190°C	Gas Mark 5 (moderate)
400°F	200°C	Gas Mark 6 (hot)
425°F	220°C	Gas Mark 7 (hot)
450°F	230°C	Gas Mark 8 (very hot)
475°F	240°C	Gas Mark 9 (very hot)
500°F	260°C	Gas Mark 10 (extremely hot)
Broil	Broil	Grill

Electric and gas ovens may be calibrated using celsius. However, for an electric oven, increase celsius setting 10 to 20 degrees when cooking above 160°C. For convection or forced air ovens (gas or electric), lower the temperature setting 25°F/10°C when cooking at all heat levels.

Baking Pan Sizes

Imperial / U.S.	Metric
9×1$1/2$-inch round cake pan	22- or 23×4-cm (1.5 L)
9×1$1/2$-inch pie plate	22- or 23×4-cm (1 L)
8×8×2-inch square cake pan	20×5-cm (2 L)
9×9×2-inch square cake pan	22- or 23×4.5-cm (2.5 L)
11×7×1$1/2$-inch baking pan	28×17×4-cm (2 L)
2-quart rectangular baking pan	30×19×4.5-cm (3 L)
13×9×2-inch baking pan	34×22×4.5-cm (3.5 L)
15×10×1-inch jelly roll pan	40×25×2-cm
9×5×3-inch loaf pan	23×13×8-cm (2 L)
2-quart casserole	2 L

U.S. / Standard Metric Equivalents

$1/8$ teaspoon = 0.5 ml	
$1/4$ teaspoon = 1 ml	
$1/2$ teaspoon = 2 ml	
1 teaspoon = 5 ml	
1 tablespoon = 15 ml	
2 tablespoons = 25 ml	
$1/4$ cup = 2 fluid ounces = 50 ml	
$1/3$ cup = 3 fluid ounces = 75 ml	
$1/2$ cup = 4 fluid ounces = 125 ml	
$2/3$ cup = 5 fluid ounces = 150 ml	
$3/4$ cup = 6 fluid ounces = 175 ml	
1 cup = 8 fluid ounces = 250 ml	
2 cups = 1 pint = 500 ml	
1 quart = 1 litre	